ADULT EDUCATION AND COMMUNITY ACTION

RADICAL FORUM ON ADULT EDUCATION SERIES
Edited by Jo Campling, Hillcroft College

Curriculum Theory in Adult and Lifelong Education
Colin Griffin

Learning Liberation — Women's Response to Men's Education
Jane L. Thompson

Adult Education and Community Action

ADULT EDUCATION AND POPULAR SOCIAL MOVEMENTS

TOM LOVETT, CHRIS CLARKE and AVILA KILMURRAY

CROOM HELM
London & Canberra

©1983 T. Lovett, C. Clarke and A. Kilmurray
Croom Helm Ltd, Provident House, Burrell Row,
Beckenham, Kent BR3 1AT
Croom Helm Australia, PO Box 391, Manuka,
ACT 2603, Australia

British Library Cataloguing in Publication Data

Lovett, Tom
    Adult education and community action.——(Radical
    Forum on adult education series)
    1. Community schools   Great Britain
    2. Education——Great Britain
    I. Title   II. Clarke, Chris   III. Kilmurray,
    Avila   IV. Series
    370.19'4'0941   LB2820

    ISBN 0-7099-1620-5

Printed and bound in Great Britain by
Biddles Ltd, Guildford and King's Lynn

CONTENTS

ACKNOWLEDGEMENTS

This book has been influenced and shaped by the work and ideals of various adult educators and social activists both here in Northern Ireland and abroad. A particular debt of gratitude is due to Louis Kools at the Folk High School in Bergen, Holland; Keith Jackson at the Northern College in Barnsley, Yorkshire; Bill Parkinson in the Department of Adult Education, Keele University, Staffordshire, England; Colin Kirkwood with the Workers' Educational Association in Edinburgh, Scotland; Myles Horton, John Gaventa and the staff at Highlander, New Market, Tennessee, U.S.A.; Budd Hall and the staff at the International Council for Adult Education, Toronto; Jim Lotz, Halifax, Nova Scotia, Canada.

In Northern Ireland the list of people who made the work described in this book possible is so large that it would be unfair to mention some and omit others. However this volume is dedicated to them, the numerous men and women throughout Northern Ireland, involved in the long, hard, unpublicised struggle for peace and social justice. Finally I would like to thank my two research assistants on the CARE project - and joint authors of this book - Chris Clarke and Avila Kilmurray for their enthusiasm and commitment to the work and the stimulus of their ideas; Yvonne Devine, our secretary, for dedication above and beyond the call of duty and Agnes McConway for all her hard work in typing and correcting what was a very untidy manuscript.

Tom Lovett,
The Ulster People's College,
Belfast,

EDITOR'S INTRODUCTION

The purpose of this series is to provide a forum of discussion for the whole field of adult and continuing education. With increasing pressure on traditional areas of secondary and higher education and changing employment patterns, there is a growing awareness that the continuing education of adults has a vital role to play in our society. All the books in the series are about radical thinking and practice in education in Britain and abroad. The authors are concerned with education in its widest sense, and, by implication, with the inadequacy of traditional views of education as a process which concerns only the young and which takes place only in the formal sectors.

A major focus of the series is on the consequences of social change and the need to formulate an educational response to new technologies and new economic, social and political conditions as they affect *all* members of our society. The growth and distribution of knowledge is rapidly making traditional models of education obsolete, and new learning technologies are being developed which give a greater potential than ever before to the possibilities of education as an instrument of social change, but only if we change radically our conceptions of education itself and adopt a critical view of the uses to which it could be put.

At the same time that educational ideals become more attainable through the growth of knowledge and learning technologies, economic, social, political, sexual and racial conflicts remain undiminished and often find expression in educational inequalities and injustices. The series aims to explore this paradox, to identify obstacles in the way of realising the full potential of education for all and to describe some of the initiatives being taken in the United Kingdom and abroad to try to overcome them.

This book examines the relationship between adult education and social change. It seeks to illustrate the nature of that relationship through an examination of the contemporary debate about the role of community education in local community action, using developments in Northern Ireland over the last decade as a case study. It attempts to relate this debate to earlier initiatives in this field, particularly those which sought to link adult education closely to popular movements for social change.

The response in Northern Ireland illustrates that there are a number of different models of community education with quite different and distinct social objectives, as far as social changes is concerned, which tend to become confused in practice. The educational theories of Freire and Illich have often assisted in this confusion, diverting attention away from questions of social purpose in adult education to ones of method and technique. The authors conclude that, if radical social objectives are to be pursued by adult educators, then there are grave limitations operating from traditional educational institutions and organisations. Alternative adult education institutions and movements with different and distinct social objectives, must be created to 'break the mould' and challenge the hegemony of the liberal approach to adult education and social change.

Jo Campling
Series Editor

Chapter 1

INTRODUCTION

ADULT EDUCATION AND SOCIAL CHANGE

In a society which is faced with enormous social and economic problems; technological change, rising unemployment, racial strife, crime and vandalism, poverty, major changes in social attitudes, values and living styles, adult education appears to have come of age. Increasingly we are told that we are all learners now; that education is a life-long process; that we must be educated for change; that we must learn to make better use of our increased leisure hours - particularly the unemployed or unemployable! Terms such as 'permanent', 'recurrent', 'continuing', 'life-long', are used to signify a new concept of adult education which will rise to meet the challenge of the latter part of the 20th Century. It is likely that in the 1980s adult education will take the place of social work in the 60s and community work in the 70s as the new remedy for many of our social and economic ills.

Already, in line with this development, there is more emphasis on 'client's needs', 'co-ordination of resources', 'effective delivery of services'. Adult education may be re-organised in an attempt to provide such a co-ordinated and comprehensive service. This may, in fact, produce changes for the better. However, the evidence from the social and other services is the danger that such a move would make adult education more institutionalised, more bureaucratic, unless there is strong community control. There is little evidence that the latter will occur despite the successful work of some community education projects in exploring how it might be done, particularly amongst that large section of the population which is sadly under-represented in adult education - the working class.[1]

However, even if such community control is possible the emphasis on 'education for change' often ignores the essentially political nature of many of the problems and issues facing adults today, defining them instead in terms of 'the disadvantaged', 'industrial needs', 'leisure needs'. The danger here is that adult education organisations and institutions will operate as socialisation agencies in much the same way as formal schooling. This is particularly true as far as 'the disadvantaged' are concerned, i.e. the poor, the

1

unemployed, single parent families, those living in socially deprived communities. They are often lumped together with the physically and mentally disabled. The problems they face are thus seen in terms of personal disability or inadequacy, to be remedied by basic education. They have to be taught to 'cope' with the complexities of modern family, industrial and political life. It is an approach based on a social pathology model, thus the emphasis on <u>human relations, personal interaction, group work, counselling, empathy.</u> The problem is a 'personal' one and has to be approached in these terms.

This analysis is central to a recent report from the Advisory Council for Adult and Continuing Education.[2] It epitomises this social pathology approach to adult education. The emphasis is on *adapting* to circumstances, *coping*, not challenging, the existing order of things.

'However successful people may have been in the past in adapting to deprivation and tolerating their lot, the social and economic trends of the day are making that response even less feasible. Disadvantage and alienation grow in the wake of inner-city decline, of rural isolation, of structural unemployment and the break-up of traditional home and work relationships, and the increasing complexity of administration even in those services designed to help. It is essential that basic education should be available wherever needed to counter the loss of personal dignity, the waste of human resources and the vulnerability to political extremism that hopeless unemployment can bring'.[3]

In Northern Ireland, a recent report (obviously influenced by the Advisory Council's analysis) produced by the Council for Continuing Education[4] places a similar stress on meeting industrial needs, on basic literacy, on leisure education for the unemployed, on remedial education. Social and political education is mentioned but this is seen almost entirely in terms of consumer and rights education. The important criteria of such courses is 'a potential for strengthening, through education, the effectiveness and efficiency of social institutions'.[5] The emphasis is on the *duties* and *responsibilities* of adults and the strengthening of social institutions. This is a long way from a recent report of a UNESCO conference on Adult Education which stated that the aims of adult education should be to 'develop a critical understanding of major contemporary problems and social changes and the ability to play an active part in the progress of society with a view to achieving social justice'.[6] The report goes on to stress that the highest priority should be given to the most educationally underprivileged groups within a perspective of *collective advancement* (my emphasis).

The developments briefly discussed above are indicative of the fact that adult education is becoming less marginal to the main stream of education, and increasingly regarded as an important and growing part of it. Whilst it was marginal it could afford to be more critical of existing institutions, less concerned with the 'needs' of the system. This liberal tradition has historically been the province of responsible bodies like the Workers' Educational Association and University Adult Education Departments. The provision of a broad liberal education by these bodies rested on the belief that it should provide, not only for personal development, but for active involvement in the social and political life of the nation.

This concept of liberal adult education is opposed to the remedial/consensus approach implicit in the developments outlined above. The position is essentially a pluralist one, viewing society in terms of 'competition' between various interest groups in society for power and resources. The emphasis is still on the individual and his contribution to social change, but it is also recognised that it is necessary for individuals to work with groups preparing them for the exercise of social duties and responsibilities.[7] Thus the liberal/reform tradition accepts the need to give spcial priority to the provision of adult education for the working class because of their general lack of education and weak position in the pluralist snooker game. The strong sense of social purpose in this tradition translates itself into an open commitment to the working class so that adult education can assist them to make the most of their individual talents and abilities and help them play an active role in the various groups and organisations in society.

Thus, whereas the social pathology approach views community education as a means of providing remedial education for the disadvantaged the liberal/reform tradition views it as a means of reaching the broad bulk of the working class, assisting individual growth and development *and* providing support for those engaged in the process of community action. Essentially this liberal view of education 'creates a belief that education provides the means of furthering personal benefit and fulfilment, whilst at the same time promoting social justice, equality and the integration of the diverse interests of differing groups in society'.[8]

This important and influential tradition of adult education in Great Britain has recently been criticised for its individualistic, essentially middle class, ethos; its belief that educating individuals eventually helps the broad mass of the working class; its acceptance of the prevailing pluralist ideology.[9] Much of this criticism has arisen during the last decade as it has become increasingly obvious to adult educators that the social engineering of the post war period (of which the liberal progressive adult education movement was an important part) has failed to create a more just and equitable society. The involvement of adult educators in community education and community action projects during the 70s provided the experience which, allied with modern educational research and theory, gradually began to question the traditional liberal education position. Keith Jackson, someone who has made an important contribution to this debate both in practice and theory, suggests that liberal progressives in education have failed not because they set themselves a social purpose, but 'because they reduced that purpose to a largely educational affair, thus losing much of its meaning in material terms for ordinary men and women'.[10]

As a result of this disenchantment with the liberal adult education tradition, efforts are being made to reinterpret it, or to replace it with an approach which places greater emphasis on relating education to real problems and issues, establishing closer links with

3

community action and social movements, creating an alternative adult education system which places greater stress on linking education and action. This approach belongs to a tradition of 'active' adult education which includes elements of reform, radicalism, and revolution. Examples of this tradition are to be found in Britain, Europe and North America.

EUROPEAN AND NORTH AMERICAN INITIATIVES

Waller, in an early article on adult education and community development, reminds us that adult education initiatives have, on many occasions, been linked to other activities, e.g. co-operatives in Denmark;   Scandinavian study circles with Scandinavian social democracy; American Land Grant Colleges with rural development in the U.S.A. He mentions, in this context, the Societa Umanitaria of Milan founded in 1893. 'It convened the first European conference on unemployment; the first on adult education; set up the first labour exchanges in Italy; the first co-operative housing scheme; the first institution for the rehabilitation of the unemployed;   trained co-operators;   had a large 'People's Theatre'; started the Italian People's Universities;   started the first adult education unions; promoted People's Libraries - all before 1910!'[11] It's interesting to note that, although there are obvious echoes here of recent adult education initiatives in this country Gramsci, the Italian Marxist, was very critical of the People's Universities comparing them to English merchants handing out 'trashy baubles to African negroes in exchange for gold'.[12] For him such exercises, although radical in *method*, were essentially reformist.   They would not succeed unless there was a strong link between such institutions and the masses and unless 'they had worked out and made coherent the principles and the problems raised by the masses in their practical activity, thus constituting a cultural and social bloc'.[13]

The contrast between the liberal and radical approaches in this educational tradition of active involvement in social, economic and political problems and issues is evident in North America where the European Folk High School movement was an important influence in numerous education movements. In Denmark, it had been closely associated not only with the co-operative movement but the growth of Danish nationalism and culture in the nineteenth century. However, in other Scandinavian countries it had close links with the labour movement. In the U.S.A. both were important influences in workers education in the early part of the century. In 1907 a Work People's College was established by Finnish socialists in Minnesota.[14] It was an important influence on the Labour College movement which blossomed in the U.S.A. during the 1920s.   It provided workers with hard intellectual education, within a Marxist perspective, and training in practical skills. The knowledge and experience gained in strikes and other industrial activity were not regarded as interruptions of school work but as genuine education as a result of which 'students and teachers alike bring wiser judgement and a keener sense of reality to their classes in consequence'.[15]

In some schools students and staff had to work, as well as study together, often reversing the usual roles. Special importance was attached to art and drama in the work of the schools. 'The theatre to my mind is a means to an end. Classified as art, it concerns itself in providing education; as propaganda it provides something to talk about'.[16] Students wrote, directed, produced and acted their own plays and the skills associated with drama production were included in the curriculum. The aim of the many Labour College courses is summed up in the following statement of objectives from the Work People's College - 'The school recognises the existence of class struggle in society and its courses of study have been prepared so that industrially organised workers, both men and women, dissatisfied with conditions under our capitalist system can more effectively carry on an organised struggle for the attainment of industrial demands and ultimately the realisation of a new social order'.[17] The Work People's College, and the American Labour College Movement, played an important role in the American Labour movement up to the 1930s when it eventually fell victim to pressure from conservative trade unions and government.

However, another initiative influenced by the Danish Folk High School tradition, the Highlander Folk School in Tennessee, which was established in the 1930s by a radical baptist minister, Myles Horton, has survived to this day.[18] Highlander played an important role in the growth and development of the trade union movement in Tennessee in the 1930s and more recently it played an important educational role in the Civil Rights Movement. Although Highlander was also committed to active physical involvement in the problems and issues facing people in that depressed region of the U.S.A. it was not so ideologically rigid as the Work People's College and the Labour College movement referred to above. It was deliberately vague about the exact meaning placed on its governing concepts - brotherhood, democracy, mutuality, concerted community action - letting the time and the people define them more precisely. It quickly learnt that ideology, no matter how firmly rooted in objective reality, was of no value if it was separated from a social movement of struggling people.

Its axiom was 'learn from the people and start education where they are'. It sought to educate people away from the dead end of individualism into the freedom that grows from co-operation and collective solutions to problems. Its goals were the release of the potential and energies of the people not the relief of those problems. Like the Labour Colleges it placed great stress on culture and art, particularly local working class culture. However, there was less stress on hard intellectual effort and more on education for the will and imagination and creative human relationships. Information and training were provided by linking action to intensive short-term residential workshops. This was supplemented by research support for local activists. Highlander suffered from attacks by the Ku Klux Klan and other reactionary elements in the South. In 1961 the State of Tennessee seized the school's property and revoked its charter. However it was quickly reorganised and rechartered under its present name, the Highlander Research and Education Centre, and continues

5

its work on a new site in New Market, Tennessee.

At the other end of this continuum from the revolutionary Marxist approach of the Work People's College, through the radicalism of the Highlander Centre is the Antigonish movement of Nova Scotia in Canada.[19] This was a programme of adult education, self help and co-operative development which became world famous during the 1930s. Again, as with Highlander, the Folk High School movement in Denmark was an important influence and the leading figures were clergymen, Father Moses Coady, and Father Jimmy Tompkins. Coady was the intellectual figurehead of the movement, operating from the Extension Department of St. Francis Xavier University. Tompkins was the field worker building the foundations of the movement amongst the poor people of the region in the 1920s.

Antigonish believed that reform would come about through education, public participation and the establishment of alternative institutions, i.e. co-operatives and credit unions. For Coady adult education was an agressive agent of change, a mass movement of reform, the peaceful way to social change. It was a populist movement, strongly anti-communist but with vision of a new society. This was the foundation of its educational philosophy and approach. It drew no fine distinctions between action and education. The movement was involved in actually creating co-operatives and credit unions linking them closely with a system of education support which was wide ranging including mass meetings, study clubs, radio discussion groups, kitchen meetings, short courses, conferences, leadership schools and training courses.

Although it did not embrace the Marxist analysis of the American Labour College Movement or the radical political philosophy of the Highlander Centre, the Antigonish movement did succeed in engaging large numbers of workers in an extensive educational programme linked to social action which even today would be regarded as too radical by many adult education institutions! In fact it appears that St. Francis Xavier University was not particularly happy with this active community involvement. When Coady died in 1959 the movement effectively died with him. As so often in such cases the University effectively 'institutionalised' the movement establishing a Coady International Institute to train people from the Third World in Antigonish methods, whilst remaining somewhat aloof from the continuing problems of poverty and injustice in its own region.

INITIATIVES IN GREAT BRITAIN

In Great Britain this tradition of active involvement in social movements is historically associated with the National Council of Labour Colleges. The latter, which grew out of the Plebs League and the disagreement with what was seen as the academic and reformist attitude of Ruskin, the worker's college at Oxford, was in some respects similar to the American Labour College Movement. Up until 1929 it had its own residential college and close links with the trade unions. However, echoing the American experience, as these unions became more right wing they became more a hindrance than a help! It also appears that the rigid Marxist teaching approach of the N.C.L.C. was less successful with students than the W.E.A.'s more traditional liberal approach, particularly during the 1930s when students were interested in the causes of unemployment and practical solutions.[20] The W.E.A. although less dogmatic and more 'objective' was more democratic and flexible in its teaching methods, developing a more critical, analytical approach in its students. The N.C.L.C. was a revolutionary educational movement with some very 'conservative' educational methods and techniques which often succeeded because of the high motivation of the students and their commitment to the political philosophy of the N.C.L.C. The W.E.A. was essentially a reformist movement.

However, both organisations trained successive generations of leaders for the trade union and labour movements, although they were less actively involved in seeking practical solutions on the ground than the initiatives in Europe and North America, discussed above. The W.E.A. has survived as the main provider of working class education. It placed greater stress on seeking state support for its work against the emphasis placed on independence by the Labour College movement. A recent article on the W.E.A. and the N.C.L.C. argues that this was the right approach; that it is unwise and unnecessary to ignore the possibilities of using the resources of the state; that such support did not, as the supporters of the Labour College movement argued, weaken its (the W.E.A.'s) commitment to the labour movement.[21]

That view has, until lately, been generally accepted. It has its origins in developments in workers' education in the late nineteenth century and early twentieth century which stressed the need to demand equal access to educational facilities provided by the state. This became the main feature of popular liberal politics and then of the Labour Party's educational stance. The debate between the W.E.A. and the N.C.L.C. in the early part of this century was thus, in some respects, the final battle in an older debate about independence and incorporation in workers' education which reaches back into the early part of the nineteenth century.

There was in fact a popular radical education tradition in the early nineteenth century which was closely associated with the radical political movement and sharply oppositional to all provided and centralised education, including the Mechanics Institute.[22] Benjamin King, a Chartist, commenting on the latter said: 'Mechanics Institutes were not intended to teach the most useful knowledge but to teach only as might be profitable to the unproductive. He trusted, however, we should now get working men to inquire how the produce of their labour was so cunningly and avariciously abstracted from them, and thence go on to the attainment of truth, in order to obtain, before long ..... happiness and community'.[23] This movement was much more informal, flexible and undogmatic than the Labour College movement of the early twentieth century. Educational activities e.g. communal readings, discussion groups, travelling scholars, newspapers, were closely related to other activities in the family, neighbourhood and work. There was little distinction between education and noneducation. The emphasis was on really useful knowledge and collective enterprise. The strategy was one of establishing alternatives. It was opposed to rigid dogma. Thus there were few organisational orthodoxies, little bureaucracy and little division between officials and the rank and file. It found in the life of the masses the source of the problems it set out to study and resolve. It was undogmatic because there was nothing but experience from which theory could spring. All it had was its popularity. Thus the informal and unacademic character of the education. However, education was seen as essentially political, part of a political movement, and the movement conducted an internal debate about education as a means of changing the world.

CONTEMPORARY DEVELOPMENTS

There are many similarities between aspects of this tradition of adult education (and the others in North America discussed above) and initiatives in community action and education in the late 1960s and 1970s, e.g. the emphasis on relating education more specifically to the life of the people; the concern for flexibility and informality; the attempts to provide for active community participation and control of educational provision; the efforts to create alternative provision; the concern to link education with the larger labour movement. This had led to debates about the relevance of 'community' as opposed to 'working class'; the dangers of informal education; the problem of co-option by the state; the role of education in social and political movements; the conflict between individual and collective advancement in the process of social and political change.[24]

This debate is well summed up in a Council of Europe evaluation of pilot experiments in this field in Europe.[25] It draws a distinction between collective education for individual development and collective education for individual *and* collective development: 'whereas the aim of social advancement is to reduce individual inequalities but the social environment which produced them is left intact (on the assumption that those inequalities are due to an inadequate education effort on the part of individuals, or the state, or to inequality of education gifts) the aim of collective advancement is to give individual education and at the same time influence the social context in which the individual lives. An effort is made to involve as many persons as possible in the education campaign. It will always be based on the concrete problems encountered by communities in real situations ..... *without collective advancement there can be no genuine individual advancement but only uprooting'.*[26]

The report especially recommended the Dutch Folk High School system as a prime example of collective education for collective advancement, linking education to social action by working in various communities and providing a residential educational element. It suggests that this system is helping to create an educational underground, separate from existing provision and asks the question: 'Can it be said ..... that side by side with individual education a system of collective education which pursues complementary and

8

distinct objectives is appearing, or are we confronted with the beginnings of a system of continuing education for adults which will supersede the former in due course?"[27] It concludes that, whatever the answer, there is a strong trend towards this sort of work and that it should be studied in more detail.

The proliferation of community education projects, community arts, workshops, community research and information centres, often allied with a variety of community action initiatives concerned with a wide range of social and economic issues at local level, bears witness to the strength and variety of this trend. Its strength is underlined by the importance attached to it by a number of adult education agencies and in reports prepared by international bodies like the Council of Europe referred to above.

The International Council for Adult Education, for instance, has embarked on an international project in participatory research, involving groups in four continents. The project focuses on the active involvement of the people themselves in researching issues and problems relevant to their lives in their community and work. In a working paper on the project, it is stressed that 'the research process should be part of a total educational experience which serves to establish community needs and increase awareness and commitment within the community ..... its object should be the liberation of human creative potential and the mobilisation of human resources for the solution of human problems'.[28] Of course such a process is not new in adult education even in the liberal tradition. It can be criticised for its naivete: its belief that research alone can bring about change; its stress on researching the community rather than those responsible for making the decisions which affect the community. However, that debate is going on within the project and is indicative of the general reassessment of the role of adult education in social and political education which is taking place in adult education circles.

Another report published by the Council of Europe stresses the need to considerably broaden the definition of art and culture to encompass, not only initiatives in community art and media, but also those 'cultural' activities designed to allow people to play a larger and more active role in their society. 'Culture is now a frankly political area. From another standpoint, it has become crystal clear that if the great mass of the people are to make a cultural democracy for themselves, a prime objective of any development policy must be the promotion of political awareness amongst them so that they can take what is, in the broadest sense, political action to achieve command of their own culture and control of the socio-economic forces which affect it, surmounting the crises of a world in crisis. Political competence, social commitment and community participation are among the essential characteristics of a man of culture'.[29] This is rather high sounding, though probably no more so than some of the comments of the early nineteenth century radical educators quoted above!

However the Council has promoted a variety of experiments in community arts over the last decade and published numerous reports

9

and assessments of its work. It must be said though that often the practice does not live up to the rhetoric. There is a certain woolliness in the analysis of social problems and injustices personified in the following statement from the author in his introduction: 'I believe in the desirability and feasibility of a liberal and egalitarian society, I do not see this in terms of this or that constitution or these or those political and economic structures, but in terms of a new life of human relationships and social behaviour'.[30] In essence, it is a reassertion of the liberal assumptions about art and culture and more concerned to broaden the definition of adult education to include a range of 'cultural' activities.

Finally a recent report by the Universities Council for Adult Education in Great Britain on Education for Participation reaserts the need to consider seriously the role of political education.[31] Referring to the Hansard Report on Political Education (which stresses the ne ed for education in political literacy in schools to proceed through examining issues rather than conventional 'citizen education'), it points out that the limitations of the classroom and the age of the audience make this sort of political education essentially an adult education task. The report emphasises the important role adult education has to play in a revitalised and participating democracy and stresses that it will cause educators to question the nature of education and the basis of existing institutions.

The concern throughout the report is on relating education to real life situations, and on the role of community education in this process. It recognises that work with community groups poses, in an acute form, several of the problems which occur in other aspects of adult education for participation, i.e., very demanding, difficult to justify in conventional terms, raises sensitive political questions. Nevertheless the group felt that such work was profoundly important and was the basic education element of education for participation, demanding more of educationalists than conventional adult education. This could mean providing practical assistance, e.g. equipment, typewriters, duplicating machinery, video etc., for community groups, or creating new sorts of learning material (particularly utilizing the media) suitable for work with adults in this field. However, although the report stresses the potential of local radio, it admits that it has not yet fulfilled expectations that it would stimulate local democracy. Finally the report places special emphasis on the role of university adult education departments in this field and the need to see themselves, and their institutions, as resources for the community. This is in the line with developments in U.S.A., where community action has mushroomed into a nationwide movement.[32] One of the reasons for the success of the variety of groups involved in this movement is the extensive network of research, information, education and training resources linked into the community action movement.

This book is an account, and an assessment, of the work of one university adult education institute in Northern Ireland which has attempted to act as such a resource for community action in this strife-torn and deprived region. Here, over the last ten years, there has been a proliferation of community activity similar in many respects to developments in Great Britain and U.S.A.[33] Education for participation may appear out of place in such a situation. However, an U.C.A.E. quote from De Toequeville is, we believe, an appropriate response to this reaction: 'When I am told that the laws are weak and the population is wild, that passions excited and virtue is paralyzed and that in this situation it would be madness to think of increasing the rights of the people, I reply it is for these very reasons that they should be increased'.[34]

Finally, in line with Keith Jackson's contention that the contradictions of liberal education can best be overcome by a constant re-interpretation of education practice in the light of theory,[35] this book is offered as one contribution to that praxis which attempts to put the work described in an historical context. The latter has been briefly outlined in this introduction. It forms the background to the more personal development of theory and practice in community education and action, over the last decade, discussed in the following chapters.

NOTES

1. See for example, T. Lovett, *Adult Education, Community Development and the Working Class*. (Ward Lock, London, 1975); C.S. McConnell, *The People's Classroom - A Scottish Case Study on Community Controlled Adult Education*. (James Watt College, Greenock, 1979); D. Rowlands, F. Gaffakin, S. Griffiths, and D. Ray, *Report of a Community Education Project 1976-1978*, (Department of Further Professional Studies, Queens University, Belfast, 1979).

2. *A Strategy for the Basic Education of Adults*, (published and distributed by the Advisory Council for Adult and Continuing Education).

3. Quoted by N. Keddie in, 'Adult Education: an ideology of individualism', in *Adult Education for a Change*, Ed. J.L. Thompson (Hutchinson & Co. Ltd., London, 1980), p. 60.

4. *Continuing Education in Northern Ireland - A Strategy for Development*. (A discussion paper published and distributed by the Northern Ireland Council for Continuing Education, 1980).

5. Ibid., p. 25.

6. *Recommendations on the Development of Adult Education*, (Paper published by the General Conference of UNESCO meeting in Nairobi 1976), p. 2.

7. For an analysis of the distinction between the conservative, liberal and radical views of adult education, see: J.E. Thomas and G. Harries-Jenkins. 'Adult Education and Social Change'. *Studies in Adult Education*, Vol. 7, No. 1, April, 1975.

8. Quoted by Jane Thompson in 'Adult Education and the Disadvantaged' in Thompson, op. cit.

9. Ibid.

10. Ibid., p. 11.

11. P. Du Sautoy and D. Waller, 'Community Development and Adult Education', *International Review of Community Development*

No. 8, 1961, p. 46.

12. *Selections from the Prison Notebooks of Antonio Gramsci.* Edited and translated by Quintin Hoare and Geoffrey Smith. (Laurence & Wishart, London 1973). p. 330.

13. Ibid., p. 330.

14. J. Altenbaugh and R.G. Paulston, 'Work People's College: A Finnish Folk High School in the American Labour College Movement', *PAEDAGOGICA HISTORICA - International Journal of the History of Education* XVIII/2 1978.

15. Quoted in: J. Altenbaugh, *'The Relationship of Work and Education in the American Labour College Movement'.* (Paper presented to the History of Education Society, Chicago, October, 1978), p. 11.

16. Altenbaugh and Paulston, Op. cit., p. 224.

17. Ibid., p. 243.

18. F. Adams and M. Horton. *Unearthing Seeds of Fire - The Idea of Highlander*, (J.F. Blair, Publisher, N. Carolina, 1975).

19. J. Lotz. 'The Antigonish Movement', in *Understanding Canada; Regional and Community Development in a New Nation*, (N.C. Press, Toronto, 1977).

20. G. Brown. 'Independence and encorporation: The Labour College Movement and the Workers' Educational Association before the Second World War', in *Adult Education for a Change*.

21. Ibid.

22. R. Johnston. ''Really Useful Knowledge': Radical education and working class culture, 1790-1848', in *Working Class Culture*, J. Clarke, C. Critcher and R. Johnson, (Eds.), (Hutchinson, London, 1980).

23. Ibid., p. 85

24. Jane L. Thompson, op. cit.

25. Council of Europe, *'Permanent Education - Evaluation of Pilot Experiments', Interim Report*, (Council for Cultural Co-operation Steering Group on Permanent Education, Strasbourg, 1974).

26. Ibid., p. 53.

27. Ibid., p. 63.

28. B.L. Hall, *Creating Knowledge: Breaking the Monopoly*, (Working Paper No. 1., Participatory Research Project, International Council for Adult Education, Toronto), p. 11.

29. J.A. Simpson, *Towards Cultural Democracy*, (Council for Cultural Co-operation. Council of Europe, Strasbourg, 1976). p. 34.

30. Ibid., p. 8.

31. Universities Council for Adult Education, *Working Party Paper on Education for Participation*, (U.C.A.E., 1980).

32. J. Perlman, 'Grassrooting the system', in *Social Policy* (U.S.A.) Sept./Oct. 1976; also 'Grassroots empowerment and government response'. *Social Policy*, Sept./Oct., 1979.

33. T. Lovett and R. Percival. 'Politics, Conflict and Community Action in Northern Ireland', in *Political Issues and Community Work*, P. Curno (Ed.) (Routledge and Kegan Paul, London, 1978).

34. *Education for Participation*, p. 6.

35. Jane L. Thompson, op. cit.

Chapter 2

COMMUNITY ACTION AND SOCIAL CHANGE

Introduction
In this chapter, we shall try to set out, in general terms, what community action comprises: where it comes from, the context in which it operates and the highly contradictory purposes it serves. We shall look briefly at the social and political setting of the post-war years and then at the effects which that had, specifically within working class communities. The account given here will be based predominately upon the British experience, where the issues related to social class are relatively clear cut, but will emphasise features common to most developed western economies. The following chapter will then deal with the role of adult education in community action before turning to look at the Northern Ireland experience in community action and education.

COMMUNITY ACTION

Popular Democratic Activity - The Background
Community action and similar phrases became very much vogue terms during the 1970's, thrown around loosely in discussion, meaning different things to different people. As far as we are concerned here, community action is a category of collective social action, based in working class residential areas, to tackle a wide range of issues arising outside the traditional places of employment. It is therefore to be distinguished from industrial action taken by trade unionists and from the electoral activities of formal political parties. It is also separate from the statutory social services run by state welfare bodies. However, the relationship between community action and those other kinds of activities is a central point of debate amongst the action groups. Many community activists are striving for some sort of organic unity between their own groups and both trade unions and sympathetic political parties; others are altogether hostile to party politics and view unions as part and parcel of the bureaucratic centralisation, from which many of their grievances derive. So, although it is useful to mark out the boundaries of community action as a conceptual distinction, we have not been in the business of policing those boundaries to exclude other kinds of social activist from

the exercises we have tried to organise.

The main areas of concern for community action groups have been housing, communal space and halls, welfare rights, unemployment, vandalism, services for the young and the aged, recreation and leisure facilities, transport, education, health and arts and writing workshops. The main localities for this kind of action have been old, inner city areas and urban housing estates. The most common initial impetus for groups to become active and attract support has been a combination of housing problems and inadequate social facilities. Housing has meant urban renewal (slum clearance, redevelopment, re-location and rehabilitation) in the inner city and rents, repairs and maintenance on the newer estates. It has also included property speculation and homelessness. Social facilities have revolved around the decline in localised services for shopping and entertainment, a decline in standards of welfare services generally and a growing sense of disorder on the streets.

Across all those issues, there has been a common thread: a demand for more control over the daily social life of the areas concerned. That cuts across all the differences of politics, of strategy and tactics, and of sectional interest. The action groups express a collective dissatisfaction with existing services and a diminishing confidence in the institutions responsible for providing them. There is an increasing mistrust of municipal and corporate power and a resolution to enforce upon its holders more accountability to the demands of particular localities. In this sense, what we have witnessed, from the mid-1960's onwards, has been a burgeoning of democratic activity in working class communities. The effectiveness, the direction, and even the purpose of that activity has varied considerably not only from place to place, where circumstances impose different demands upon people, but within particular areas, where sharp conflicts have frequently emerged. Nevertheless, we only have to compare the recent trend in such collective activity with the profound passivity of the 1950's to see the remarkable growth that has occurred.

Community action remains a minority activity and, where moments of confrontation occur, powerful institutions usually have little difficulty in resisting the pressure imposed upon them, maintaining their own priorities in the face of loud complaints. But the significant thing is that a previously passive, compliant minority are now making their voices heard. They can no longer be taken entirely for granted. Institutions of all kinds, from state housing authorities to multinational corporations, have to pay attention to a political irritant. Most of them have developed community affairs and public relations strategies for preventing the irritation turning into a disease.

Through all the important differences that divide action groups, that remains the most illuminating way of conceptualising what is happening. Community action is part of a general political resistance by working class people to the activities of state and corporate power and to some of the wider effects of the logic and structure of that power in the course of daily life. In most cases, it is not a particularly coherent or effective form of resistance. It pulls in many, often contradictory directions, by no means all of them progressive. It is frequently short-lived. It lacks a consistent credible strategy for enforcing its various demands upon the centres of power and it commonly fails even to conceive of such a problem, remaining confined within the cells of a militant localism. But it is active. It does touch a number of raw nerves amongst working class populations and thus gains acquiescent support. It is, for the most part, driven by working class people (although the role of sons and daughters, returning home as part of a new intelligentsia, in influencing the character of the action should not be overlooked). And, it used not to happen at all.

Throughout the long economic boom, up to the mid-1960's, there was a prevailing orthodoxy in academic and official circles which defined democracy as a system of competing political elites, with the vast majority of the population politically inert between elections. Political activity by the masses, who were commonly seen as ignorant and unreasoning, was considered positively dangerous. Correlations were drawn between a politically assertive populace and authoritarian regimes. The U.S^A^ was held up admiringly as the model of liberal democratic stability and rarely more than half of its electorate even bothers to turn out to vote in its elections. In most of the western capitalist countries claiming to be democracies, the great majority of the people wanted nothing to do with regular political activity. If that seemed to go against some of the elevated ideals of democratic theorists, like Rousseau and Mill, it nevertheless worked admirably well. What people wanted was the system to come up with the goods; they didn't want to be bothered with actually running it themselves.

By the end of the 1960's, 'participation' had become something of a key word in the democratic vocabulary. From a number of different premises, criticism was voiced of competitive elites. Some suggested that popular passivity, though apparently efficient in getting things done, was not in the long run conducive to stability; it was argued that political ignorance and social prejudices were born out of political inertia or encouraged by it and that such imperfections in the general culture of a society threatened to undermine even a semblance of democracy. Others claimed that there was nothing democratic about what was later referred to as an 'elective dictatorship', in which political elites competing in regular elections did nothing to remove class divisions which were inimical to genuine democracy.

Such arguments were less important than the changing social practices from which they were distilled. For one reason or another, from the mid-sixties on, organised social and political activity was encouraged in working class areas, both by agencies of the state and by a variety of people at the grass roots. As far as the state was concerned, community development, as it came to be called, started during the sixties as a straightforward modernisation of social work, designed to deal with the more intractable aspects of 'urban deprivation', which the standard battery of welfare services seemed unable to cope with. Participation at that stage implied mutual support amongst the poor and the 'socially handicapped', in an effort to raise the morale of the most depressed sections of the population. By the mid-1970's, community development had been elevated to a larger role in general urban management. As budgets were increasingly squeezed and the legitimacy of city authorities became less obviously secure, some statutory services were gradually off-loaded on to community groups and families and efforts were made to win popular consent for the local state policies by involving working class representatives in marginal aspects of decision-making. Meanwhile, with various degrees of independence from state initiatives, action groups were appearing throughout this period in working class residential areas all over the western world. It is the inter-play of those different initiatives and the interests they represented that has shaped community action since the mid-1960's.

Many factors are at stake here: political and economic structures in the widest sense, changes in working class culture, specific elements of social and economic policy, the character of social democratic and trade union politics, etc. We can only consider a few of them here.

'De-subordination'

In a recent paper, Ralph Miliband characterised the general trend, of which community action is a part, as a process of 'de-subordination'[1]. His argument begins in 1945. After the Second World War, the British Government reached a settlement with its working class constituents, which guaranteed or promised certain material benefits in return for popular compliance in the necessary disjunctions of post-War reconstruction. The main elements of that promise were full employment, wider access to social mobility, especially through education, a rising standard of living and the safety net of a comprehensive welfare state. Never again would the cruelties of a chaotic economic market, prone to booms and slumps, be visited upon the people who had suffered so much in the thirties and whose sterling efforts had won the War. People would have to be patient, because a new world would not rise out of the ashes overnight. They would also have to be quiet, because repeated disruptions of the State's whole enterprise would only postpone or even jeopardise the new Jerusalem. Immediate demands would have to be postponed for the time being. The high social aspirations engendered by the solidarity of the war years would eventually be satisfied if only working class people trusted their political representatives, left economic and political management up to them and accepted a subordinate position in the course of events.

By the mid-1960's, with a Labour administration returned to power in Britain after more than a decade of Conservative government, the promise was wearing very thin. A generation with no personal experience of the thirties had come of age, wage restraint was constantly being imposed, welfare services were beginning to falter, a long economic boom was coming to an end, the pressures of industrial work discipline were getting worse rather than better, and still there was no sign of marked improvement in popular democratic control over events. The world of working class people in the 1960's simply wasn't Shangri La and seemed not even to be approaching it. Subordination was less and less acceptable as a price to pay. The settlement began to fall apart.

At that point, popular democratic activity started to come out of its slumbers. A revived shop stewards' movement development in centres of large-scale industrial employment. White collar employees flocked into new unions. More and more women, drawn into the workforce by the labour shortage created in the 50's economic boom, joined trade unions, many playing an active part. Strikes and other forms of industrial dispute became commonplace in sectors where they were previously unknown, with spectacular examples like the seamen, Leeds clothing workers and Pilkington's employees.[2] A number of the car firms, whose workers had been quiet for years, embarked upon campaigns of industrial militancy and, in general, workers whose employers had joined the stream of mergers and amalgamations, encouraged by state bodies, decided to strike for new demands, like parity between merged companies, and found that they had a very potent weapon. The more centralised manufacturing industry became, the more sectors of the economy became profoundly interdependent, with the result that a shutdown in one plant or company caused wider and wider disruption to industry as a whole. The rapid growth in scale of industrial employers seemed to be stalked by a growing vulnerability to their employees' non-co-operation. Management's 'right to manage' was increasingly problematic, as organised workers laid down more active conditions for their consent. The state was driven to try to introduce legislation to curb the power of the shop floor, by strengthening the authority of the full-time trade union leadership and curtailing the right to industrial action, but initially it met solid resistance and had to back off.

At the same time, immigrants, drawn into Britain by the same labour shortage, formed groups to resist the pressure for immigration controls and to defend themselves against racialist attacks. Pressure groups on housing and poverty were formed. Tenants' associations were resuscitated and other kinds of community action set in motion, some in the wake of news from America, where it was flourishing. Students in higher education began occupations and marches (culminating, in France, in the May 1968 crisis) and decided to confront the Labour Government head-on over its abject support for the American invasion of Vietnam. The Labour Party declined at the grass roots, losing many potential recruits to new splinter parties to its left (as also did the Communist Party, after the Soviet invasion of Czechoslovakia), to community action and single-issue politics, or to political oblivion. Following the example of the Campaign for Nuclear Disarmament, at the beginning of the decade, single-issue campaigns were mounted on questions like apartheid in South Africa and environmental issues at home.

By the end of the 1960's, an array of vocal and persistent minority groups had succeeded in unseating the political quiescence of the previous twenty-odd years. Even the bureaucratic hierarchies of the trade union movement, which had done so much to police the popular inertia of the previous period, were drawn into an active undermining of the government by the end of the decade and would carry that over into the early part of the 1970's.

The 1970's saw numerous important changes, yet none of them effectively suppressed this mood of de-subordination. On the contrary, more and more sections of the population decided to unsettle the consensus so assiduously promoted by the state. Of them all, the most significant impact was made by women. They were represented by a strange assortment of groups, most of them militant, many of them relatively small. What they collectively composed was a movement of considerable historical importance. It was the movement as a whole, rather than its constituent parts or even its particular achievements, which will probably be seen to have had the most profound effect upon social and political life, not only in Britain, but throughout the advanced industrial nations. Specific gains for women's interests were actually comparatively sparse. But the political culture as a whole was visibly marked. The women's movement threw down a challenge with large implications for any future political settlements. Even the welfare state, in the original Beveridge proposals, had been premised upon a domestic incarceration of women. After the 1970's, it will be much less easy for the state to re-impose female domesticity. The de-subordination of women has still hardly even begun, but another important step has been made towards it, with considerable consequences, not just for the state, but also for the labour movement generally and particularly for community action.

In other respects, however, the major developments of the seventies were less propitious for popular democratic advance. The two main objectives of that kind of political agitation, improvement of living standards and enlargement of democratic control, received major setbacks of an extremely worrying kind. A whole approach to economic management, upon which full employment and the welfare state were based, was abandoned, with nothing to replace it except pre-War and even older strategies. Paralleling that, the instruments of state control, which labourism and social democracy had heralded as tools for expanding democracy and approaching socialism, continued to degenerate into an inflated statism with exactly the opposite effects. By the end of the decade, democracy was on the run, the labour movement was weak and some very old-fashioned political sabre-rattling had been revived.

The State and Economic Management

Baldly stated, what the 1970's witnessed was the collapse of the economic management policies which formed the bedrock of the welfare state. The welfare state services themselves cannot survive that loss, unless an alternative economic strategy is found. In Britain and the other developed capitalist economies, the state was not prepared to adopt an alternative which would safeguard the welfare state. Instead, the services developed since 1945 would, in large part, be sacrificed upon the altar of the 1930's, now re-christened 'monetarism'. The high drama of this turn-around was disguised in Britain by the fact of it being a Labour government that made the giant leap into the past. But the colour of the administration makes no difference. The fact remains, that, in the summer and autumn of

1976, the Callaghan Government threw the economic foundations of the post-War political settlement out of the window. The manner in which this was done would repay considerable attention, because most of the aspirations of community action took the long drop simultaneously. We can only note it briefly here.[3]

During that eventful summer and autumn, the British Government was unceremoniously forced by its dominant capitalist partners to accept a multi-billion dollar loan from the International Monetary Fund. It was not so much that such loan facilities have strings attached; it would be more accurate to describe them as a noose. The executioner referred to his victim as 'the soft under-belly of public expenditure', which was otherwise translated as 'a euphemism for the Welfare State'. More than £5,000 million had to be cut from public expenditure over a period of two years.

It didn't augur well for community action. The groups could hardly afford to wave goodbye to £5 billion of welfare spending and yet the pressure they could exert to prevent it didn't amount to the tiniest flea-bite in such august company. In fact, the whole episode, the forming of long-term national economic policy, from which so much else follows, was concealed from public gaze and attempts were made subsequently to keep it secret. All the public saw was the Chancellor of the Exchequer rushing unexpectedly from the VIP lounge at London Airport to make a defiant and angry speech at the Labour Party Conference, to prevent the passing of a resolution calling for nationalisation of the major banks and a number of other policy resolutions, which many community groups have considered essential to the fulfilment of their basic demands. Behind the scenes, something akin to a coup d'etat was taking place (with the complicity of the Labour Government) and many of the community action's most fundamental demands fell amongst its sacrificial victims.

The melodrama of '76 is instructive in many ways. It highlights the political economic conditions under which working class democratic organisation has to operate. Community action was born out of discontent with the post-1945 political economic settlement, the politics of social democracy and the welfare state, the 'mixed economy' and municipal welfarism. It was able to gain support and win concessions, in terms of both resources and popular consultation in political decision-making, under the conditions of that settlement. The concessions were mostly quite marginal. The dominant trends of state and corporate policy were scarcely affected by them, except insofar as more attention had to be given to winning consent from a much less passive working class populace. Nevertheless, small victories at the margin encouraged the activists to press on and sustain their demands. Until, that is, the rules of the game were radically altered. The 1970's saw successive victories for those interests which were pressing, with much greater resolve and vigour, in exactly the opposite direction: against enlarged municipal services, against rising wage-incomes (or a rising share of wages in the gross domestic product), against expanded public consultation in decision-making and against popular democratic resistance of all kinds. The fact that some of these interests simultaneously sprinkled taxdeductable tit-bits in the direction of community groups, through organisations such as the Action Resource Centre,[4] was just a public relations exercise, which made no difference to the primary pressure which they imposed upon the state.

Community action groups have suffered greatly from this. As a whole, the minority of people who were prepared to put their efforts into it were forced back into the more conservative forms of recuperative community work, where their willing hands are employed full-time in saving the most deprived and helpless members of the community, abandoned by shrinking state services, from utter collapse. Lacking a coherent programme of resistance, the most radical aspirations of community action were faced with general defeat. Many activists have become demoralised and many have wondered what on earth has been going on. No sooner had a tide of small, but significant advances been made and a real sense of political movement emerged, than the whole enterprise received a succession of crippling body blows. Groups no longer haggled, campaigned and fought for the establishment of better facilities, like nursery schools; suddenly, they were fighting against closures of facilities, rapidly rising costs and large-scale redundancies in the very services they wished to see expanded. And it simultaneously became apparent that effective political decisions were receding further and further, not only from the grass roots, but equally from all the elected authorities.

It would be too superficial an explanation to see responsibility for these reversals residing solely within the British or any other national government. What the situation in '76 exposed was the underlying flaws of the post-War solution to the competing economic demands of labour and capital. The combination of Keynesian economic management and social democratic politics, though relatively benign in the 1950's and 60's failed to establish a secure foundaiton for long term progress towards prosperity and failed especially to deal with the inequalities of social class. Concentrating upon redistribution of the fruits of capitalist production, the Keynesian-social democratic strategy did little to change the method of production itself, from which class division essentially derived. As faith in that strategy has steadily declined, the search for alternatives has been renewed.

Changes in Working Class Life

If such large scale trends in political economic affairs provide the background setting for popular democratic activity, its character, form and diversity derive from more immediate circumstances. At its height, the Keynesian-social democratic strategy succeeded in revamping ailing, war-torn economies and lifted much of working class life on to a new plane of existence. But many of the consequences of this partially healthy development have been far from comforting to working class people.

In general terms, the conditions of working class community life have been thoroughly changed and much of that change has been an unsettling experience. A range of social institutions and daily practices, which had been established since the 1920's and which provided security and meaning to people's lives, have been undermined or eliminated. The closeness of many neighbourhoods has gone. Familiar roles within family life have been completely unseated. Aspects of social life that previously were organised around membership of familiar groupings have been transformed into parts of a commerical leisure industry. Working class life as a whole has been invaded by undemocratic state bureaucracies, on the one hand, and by rapid commercialisation on the other. Working class people have become the mass market for commerce and profit-making of all kinds; people have increasingly found themselves treated as consumers, where once they felt they were in a place of their own. This is not a unique historical process; the conditions of working class life have been repeatedly changed, since the Industrial Revolution and the creation of industrial urban life. Forms of communality and shared existence have certainly emerged from the recent changes, particularly in times of crisis. They are, nevertheless, new forms of social life and have had to be constructed in the wake of post-war developments.

It is central to the argument in the rest of this chapter that we are clear about the notion of 'construction'. Looking back on earlier historical periods, it can appear that populations of different kinds adapt somehow automatically to changes in their circumstances. Some kind of positive arrangement of social life seems simply to emerge, like a collective reflex, out of both adversity and change. When a national war occurs, people suddenly rally together. This is a mystification. The conditions of sensible communal life do not have a momentum of their own; they have to be created by particular men and women. Communal arrangements have to be constructed by some amongst the relevant population going out of their way to make them happen. Social order is a human creation, not a natural one. As far as working class people are concerned, social order is, in large part, imposed upon them by members of a different social class; that is one of the defining characteristics of class division. But there is almost always another kind of social order within working class communities, imposed or composed, fought over and persistently changed by people living within those communities. This social order has its own values, rituals, rules of conduct, sanctions against offenders, hierarchies, allocation of social roles, etc., which stand in an uncertain relation to the dominant order, sometimes and in some places very much subordinate or subservient, elsewhere radically defiant, usually a mixture of both. This immediate social order is very important in any community and especially so where people are threatened by insecurity. It is constantly being worked at and worked over by a minority of activists of many colours. To call such people unrepresentative of the community as a whole is, in one sense, accurate. But they are nevertheless vital contributors to community life. If no one undertook to organise and encourage ordered collective practices, a humane and tolerable communality would be virtually impossible. While it is undoubtedly true, as Piven and Cloward[5] claim, that outbreaks of general disorder and street rioting can lead to positive gains for subordinate sections of a society, such gains can only be beneficial in the long run if they contribute to a more enlightened social order. Persistent breakdowns in communality are generally attractive only to those who escape the consequences.

However, the character of working class social order is very much a political matter. It is an arena of patient organisation, of dispute and struggles, within which conflicting political interests contend. As working class social life goes through the kind of upheavals that have occurred since 1945, the battles to secure specific kinds of order are intensified and that is where community action has found a place.

The main changes of the post-War period can be quite briefly summarised. Pre-War patterns of both geographically defined community life and family structures have been systematically undermined. As far as the locality is concerned, two main factors have effectively destroyed earlier neighbourhood solidarities. First, successive and accelerating reconstructions of industry have repeatedly shifted employment from one place to another. The search for profitable investment opportunities has led entrepreneurs to move their capital around, both within nation states and around the world, at an increasing speed. That makes geographical stability impossible. There has been a premium upon the mobility of labour. After the war, workers in declining areas like Clydeside and South Wales were drawn or driven to places like Corby, to work in the new steel mill. Twenty-odd years later, the mill is closing and workers and their families must move on again. Without an effective regional policy, an imposibility under market conditions, people must follow the jobs, like camp followers in an industrial war. This has forced many hundreds of thousands of people to build new social relations with neighbours and workmates at least once and sometimes twice or more within a generation. There can be little doubt that this process makes tightly integrated community life impracticable. The British Community Development Project reports have provided abundant evidence of the destructive effects of that kind of industrial change.[6]

Secondly, the laudable objective of urban renewal has been tackled in a manner which took little or no account of the way it might disrupt important human relationships. Large numbers of people have moved into better accommodation and the general housing stock of some areas has been greatly improved. But an enormous amount of grief has resulted along the way, particularly amongst the aged.[7] People have felt themselves blackmailed into moving to places which they positively abhorred and innumerable settled relationships within families and neighbourhoods have been damaged. A good deal of official effort has more recently been devoted to trying to ameliorate this process and that can be counted for as one of the successes of communal resistance. But much that was distinctly life-enhancing within working class communities has already gone by the board.

To a large extent, blaming the municipal planners for this bureaucratic dictation has been misplaced. Planners, housing authority officers and even city councillors have had strictly limited room for manoeuvre. The logic of municipal policy had to give priority to finance and encouraging private industry to invest in new plant within their boundaries. Municipal finances have been saddled with inflated debt burdens and a declining rate income, and private ownership of development land and city property, often for the purpose of commodity speculation, has severely hampered even the most democratic local authority. The same underlying processes have encouraged city councils to adopt rigid zoning policies and concentration of specific urban activities like shopping and leisure facilities within single, large-scale complexes, usually a considerable distance from the homes of most shoppers. The neighbourhood corner ship, which used to serve as the focus for numerous social contacts, has progressively disappeared, not so much as an autonomous planning policy but more as a result of state support for the general trend towards capital concentration within the service and distribution sectors of the economy. The logic of private capital investment has worked consistently against the protection of settled urban villages, which used to surround the working class community and governments which give priority to profitable private enterprise have had to support that trend.

Recreation and leisure activities have gone through a parallel transformation. The leisure industry as a whole has been one of the fastest growing and most profitable sectors of capital investment and its success has been founded upon an invasion of working class social life. That is not to imply that the change is all bad, but it is apparent that many moments of working class life that used to be private, or express a close mutuality amongst neighbours, have become much more clearly commercialised. Fewer and fewer leisure pursuits are free of payment; there is a greater range of things to go to, at least in the more prosperous towns and cities, but they are generally more functional and less familiar.

As far as the family is concerned, the two main trends have been towards isolation and internal fracture. The main tendency to isolation has come from the dissolution of neighbourhood supports, both from the extended family and from a relatively stable local community. Urban renewal has rarely catered for social groups larger than the nuclear family. New housing has been designed with no appreciation of alternative possibilities, of more communal forms of habitation. Yet attempts to meet the demands of young couples for a house of their own need not have precluded a wider choice of social living arrangements, allowing, for instance, successive generations of families to occupy self-contained units within larger blocks or single parents to share certain communal resources. Flexibility of that kind would probably have required a float of excess housing, which would have cost more, so we return to the problems of inadequate housing finance. But the effect remains: a strengthening of the nuclear form at the expense of alternatives.

This has both followed and reinforced a longer term trend in technology and social practice towards a home-centred society. For a variety of reasons, potentially liberating technologies have been manufactured in forms specifically geared to satisfaction of social needs within each individual home. To take advantage of such mechanical supports people have to embrace the general move towards isolation.

The family has been internally fractured by a number of things.

of Report '88 - '89 TRENDS

23

Post-war youth has acquired a financial independence, which though limited, sets modern adolescence apart from its pre-war pattern. A considerable part of national economies are now devoted entirely to the youth market. And a bewildering (to parents) series of youth sub-cultures have attracted the affiliation of a high proportion of working class young people. Adolescence seems to have become a more distinctly separate time of life, with a world all its own.[8]

Women have gained both more independence and additional burdens. The drive for cheap unskilled labour in the growing service sector and some forms of manufacturing has led an increasing number of married women to take paid employment. Some state services have been provided to relieve the responsibility for child rearing, from nursery schools to social workers, although hardly replacing what was dismantled at the end of the war. At the same time, there is more anxiety about ensuring that children are brought up properly and that 'motherhood' is not neglected. This has come partly from the state and partly from manufacturers who have seen an ideology of motherhood as a convenient inducement to sell their products. On a wider front, being 'a woman' has come to mean requiring an increasing number of commerical accessories. 'Femininity', though in some senses freer, has also been more vigorously promoted. But one very obvious bonus has been the arrival of easily available contraception, which has allowed women, particularly when young, to begin to escape some of the more repressive taboos against their sexuality. In the long run, that promises to effect a permanent change in women's position within marriage.

None of these changes marks an absolute new beginning. Working class life still exhibits numerous continuities. Sexual roles remain a powerful influence over social life in general and the neighbourhood is still a focus of group identification for very many people. Social behaviour has not changed out of recognition. But the context in which familiar practices occur is different. In particular, the values are different. There is more emphasis upon individual achievement and freedom, more tolerance of indulgence and express-iveness, a weaker identification with communal interests. Much has changed for the good, but there is also a sense of loss and a pervasive belief that the authorities are still taking people for a ride, whatever the party in power. And that sense of powerlessness is particularly acute for the weaker sections of the working class, long-term claimants, the aged, the unemployed, the disabled and others. These people have watched the power of the state grow, often in the name of socialism and working class interests, and have received very little out of the process. Now they see the state withdrawing services, but maintaining a big presence in other ways, not protectng them any more but not disappearing either. They are asked for mounting rents for poorer houses, higher fares for less efficient transport, higher charges for longer queues at the surgery, more for school meals and clothes, with only youth unemployment and aggro and trouble with the police to look forward to.

This is the seedbed of community action: working class people simultaneously encouraged and disappointed, and sometimes even frightened, by what is happening; little or no respect for dominant politicians, but no sign of a credible alternative; mistrustful of anything large-scale, wanting to capture some immediate control over events before they get any worse; isolated and genuinely uplifted when forms of lost communality can be restored; reluctant to stick their necks out and commit themselves to supporting anything that looks stupid or hopeless, but often willing to maket ime for activities and campaigns that show prospects of getting somewhere. If all that seems decidedly ambivalent then the ambivalence is mirrored in the nature of community action.

CONCLUSION

The revival of community action and other popular political organis-ations has reflected the failure of dominant political leaderships to deal with the problems of working class communities. Promises that looked plausible soon after the war are cynically dismissed in the 1980's. Small groups of working class people all over the western world (and parallelled spectacularly now in Poland) have decided to withdraw consent from established political and labour movement leaders and take matters into their own hands. As yet, this reaction lacks coherence; abundant aspirations are no match for objective setbacks. Global defeats still overwhelm the specific attempts at resistance and there are few signs of defence being transformed into demands for executive power.

Yet the crisis which confronts us in the latter part of the 20th century is not just a crisis of capitalism, in the narrowly economic sense (though it is certainly that); it is a crisis of the social and political order in a much more general sense, affecting daily life in quite intimate ways and raising grave doubts in ordinary people's minds about the whole direction of social progress and enlightenment. There is a battle going on over the way out of the crisis, over the kind of social order that will replace the one which shows signs of disinte-grating. The historically spectacular part of it is being conducted in open warfare, often in places far outside Europe, from Vietnam to southern Africa. But it is also going on much closer to home, in apparently less dramatic ways, from day to day in working class areas, where people are constantly being challenged to invent a social order and a movement which can deal with the insecurity, isolation and chaos which threatens. Community action is one of the arenas in which that battle is being fought.

At its best, it has represented an attempt to confront the dual problems of necessity and desire, as Thompson has called them[9]; the necessity of resources and the desire for a more humane, harmonious and fulfilling life. That has been its strength. Of course, innumerable community associations have scuttled into bars and clubs and halls, to evade the daunting political challenges that working class communities face, and the forces of the established order have been only too eager to encourage such leisure time retreats, just as they promoted workingmen's clubs in the 19th century. But socialists who think that devotion to politics alone is a plausible alternative are usually very disappointed with the popular response. Necessity and desire should never be separated; indeed, it has been the historical purpose of all progressive political movements to bring them together. The weakness of the working class interest in social and political affairs in the recent period has been not only a weakness of political organisation, but also a debility of communal life, which underpins a labour movement. The independence and defiance of much working class culture in the 19th and early 20th centuries has been under attack. Large events, like the British Steel strike in 1980, can reawaken that lost vigour, but it will not be reconstituted by politics alone.

The weakness of most community action has been that the participants who have emphasised mutuality and morale have had no answer to the political and economic problems except defeat and resignation, while those who have stressed working class political struggle have done little for the stirrings of communality and desire. The pendulum of popular support swings between the two, as circumstances make mutual support or political confrontation the more pressing demand. The real task of the organiser is to appreciate the force of the underlying duality and reconcile its poles.

It is in that context that adult education has a part to play. Activists need to learn about both strands of this duality: they must appreciate the need to confront insecurity and isolation, in order to raise morale; and they must acquire the skills of political and economic leadership to construct a genuinely credible alternative to the mess we presently find ourselves in. The seeds of both those skills are buried in the history of both the working class and other progressive social movements. The task of the educator is to organise activities which will draw out that heritage and sharpen up those skills.

NOTES

1. Ralph Milliband, 'A State of De-subordination' *British Journal of Sociology* Vol. XXIX, No. 4 (1878) pp. 399-409.
2. Richard Hyman's article in *Socialist Register* (Merlin Press, London, 1973).
3. For a fascinating account of this episode, see the booklet by Fay and Young *The Day the Pound Nearly Died* (available from the Sunday Times, Grays Inn Road, London).
4. A.R.C. is an organisation which channels spare management and technical staff from industrial enterprises into limited terms of work for community groups. Many of the largest corporations have loaned staff who are approaching retirement or still in the process of training, usually for a period of 6 months to 2 years. Projects assisted include a store selling seconds and second-hand goods to the population of a run-down area of Glasgow.
5. Frances Fox Piven and Richard Cloward, *Poor People's Movements* (Basil Blackwell, London, 1978).
6. See, for example, National Community Development Project *The Costs of Industrial Change* (available from Benwell Community Project, 85/87 Adelaide Terrace, Benwell, Newcastle-upon-Tyne

NE4 8BB).

7.   See Sidney Jacobs, *The Right to a Decent House* (Routledge and Kegan Paul, London, 1976);   also Gladys Elder, OAP *The Alienated: Growing Old Today* (Writers and Readers, London, 1978).

8.   Tony Jefferson et al. (eds) *Resistance Through Rituals* (Routledge and Kegan Paul, London, 1976).

9.   E.P. Thompson, *William Morris: Romantic to Revolutionary* (Merlin Press, London, 1977).

Chapter 3

COMMUNITY EDUCATION AND COMMUNITY ACTION

The role of adult education in community development and community action has aroused a great deal of debate, discussion and action by socially committed adult educators over the last decade.[1] The upsurge of initiatives in community work, community development, community organisation, community action (by voluntary bodies, social work departments, government agencies and local residents) during the late sixties and early seventies came at a time when many of those involved in adult education were questioning the role and purpose of their organisation or institution, particularly regarding the continuing failure of adult education to reach the great proportion of the working class population.[2] The 'rediscovery' of poverty and educational inequality in the sixties emphasised - if it needed emphasising - that adult education still had a role to play in compensating for the failure of the formal educational system and contributing to the struggle for social and political justice. The heady days of Supermac and 'We never had it so good' had temporarily obscured this fact.

The question of social purpose once again became a relevant and important theme for adult educators. There was increasing pressure on organisations like the Workers' Educational Association to concentrate on the needs of the working class.[3] There was also a great deal of debate and discussion about, the need to popularise knowledge, utilising aspects of working class and popular culture in adult education; the creation of a new open college for adults; broadening the scope of instrumental education (like that provided for trade unionists) to other active sections of the working class; the necessity for greater informality and flexibility in the practise of adult education.[4] As a result of this debate there was a search for new educational methods, techniques and organisational forms. Earlier initiatives in this field (like those discussed in chapter one) were, with some exceptions, forgotten in the enthusiasm for 'new' approaches to an old problem.

Important theoretical influences at the time were Bernstein, Illich and Freire. Bernstein reinforced the belief that language and culture were major barriers in attracting working class adults to education. Consequently more attention was paid to working class and popular culture.[5] Freire tended to confirm this approach with his concept of 'cultural invasion' and the importance of using every day life and experience in an educational dialogue about concrete issues and problems, linking reflection to action in a continuing praxis.[6] Illich stressed the need to de-institutionalise education, to think instead of creative and dynamic 'learning networks' utilising a variety of educational resources, formal and informal, including the skills and talents of the people themselves.[7]

At a more practical level adult educators, like their counterparts in social work and education, were influenced by the initiatives taken by the federal agencies in the U.S.A. to resolve the problems of poverty and inequality.[8] The concept of the community school and community development were important influences here. As far as the former is concerned adult educators saw the emphasis on home-school links and parental involvement in schools as opportunties for involving working class parents in relevant education meeting a real need, i.e. their children's education. The concept of the community school was viewed as an opportunity to widen the role of the school, to make it a 'community' resource, with a special stress on the provision of adult education and resources for local community action.[9]

As far as community development is concerned, many adult educators regarded its emphasis on 'effective service delivery' - co-ordinating all the relevant social, educational and welfare resources and linking them more effectively to local needs and interests - as a total learning network with adult education helping to improve communication and understanding between all those responsible for, and involved in, the search for solutions to local community problems. This view of community development was summed up in the first of the Gulbenkian Reports on community work. 'Community work is essentially concerned with affecting the course of social change through the two processes of analysing social situations and forming relationships with different groups to bring about some desirable change. It has three main aims: the first is the democratic process of involving people in thinking, deciding, planning and playing an active part in the development and operation of services that affect their daily lives: the second relates to the value for personal fulfilment of belonging in a community: the third is concerned with the need in community planning to think of actual people in relation to other people and the satisfaction of their needs as persons rather than to focus attention upon a series of separate needs and problems'.[10]

Finally the growth, at local level, of a variety of community groups and associations concerned with a wide range of issues and problems was seen as a movement of popular participation which presented opportunities for educators to get away from the restrictions of the formal class; to relate adult education more effectively to the real issues and problems facing the working class; to break down the distinction between education and action. In fact community development theorists argued that community development was essentially an educational process. 'The community development process is clearly educational. It is so recognised by men who have worked long in the field. But the process is educational in a fundamental sense that goes beyond formal teaching and disciplined

29

drill. It re-emphasises the outcomes in terms of people's lives, values, systems and competence'.[11]

It's interesting to note that Frank Milligan - a pioneer of new initiatives in adult education during the 1930's recognised the limitations of the class.[12] He established a residential centre for the unemployed which combined practical work and recreational activity with training in specific skills, involvement in drama, art and more intellectual pursuits. He was influenced by syndicalist and guild socialist ideas, particularly M.P. Follett's book 'The New State' which, echoing the emphasis today on neighbourhood community organisation stated that: 'The reason we want neighbourhood organisation is not to keep people within their neighbourhood organisations but to get them out. The movement for neighbourhood organisations is a deliberate effort to get people to identify themselves actually, not sentimentally, with a larger and larger collective unit than the neighbourhood. We may be able, through neighbourhood groups, to learn the social pressure, to learn to evolve the social will. But, the question before us is whether we have enough political genius to apply this method to city organisation, national organisation and to international organis-ation.'[13] Although Milligan was no extremist, nevertheless he was regarded as an agitator by some education officials at the time. His reply to this accusation was that too many people were too patient and that the educational system should make them discontented especially if the ways of reconstruction were left open. He quoted J.S. Mill, 'Nothing is more certain that that improvement in human affairs is wholly the work of discontented characters!'.[14]

All in all those various developments seemed to offer exciting new possibilities for adult education to play a small, but important, role in helping to create a participatory democracy, and finding solutions to the problems of social inequality and poverty by involving large sections of the working class in relevant, and meaningful, education. As a result during the late sixties and the seventies adult educators and community workers were involved in a wide variety of 'community education' initiatives.[15] Two projects which, in various ways, influenced those initiatives and the general debate about the concept of community education and its role in community action over the last decade were, the Education Priority Area Project[16] and the Vauxhall Project[17] both of which were located in Liverpool (then the Mecca of community education and development) in the late sixties and early seventies.

The Educational Priority Area Project

The Liverpool E.P.A. Project was set up in 1968 along with a number of others in England and Scotland. It was the first of the British Government's action-research projects designed to tackle the problems of poverty and educational inequality in inner cities. The E.P.A. projects were concerned specifically with the role of the primary school in the community.[18] The Liverpool project was, however, the only one with a specific adult education component, a direct result of the interest and work undertaken into the problems of working class adult education by the District Secretary of the Workers' Educational

Association in that city.[19]

The Newson Report on secondary education,[20] and the Plowden Report on primary education,[21] aroused his particular interest in the opportunities the E.P.A. project could afford the W.E.A. to involve working class parents in classes and courses concerned with their children's education - and so compliment and reinforce the work of the project in the schools. In 1969 a W.E.A. tutor-organiser was appointed to work exclusively with the E.P.A. Project team in central Liverpool.[22] From the beginning the tutor recognised that some considerable time would have to be given to exploring the area, becoming acquainted with its people and their problems, before it would become clear what sort of education was wanted or needed. Since the E.P.A. project covered an area of central Liverpool with a population of 90,000 this was not an easy task and the first year of his work was taken up almost exclusively with this process of exploration and investigation. Freire in his work has stressed that this is the essential first stage in the critical educational process: exploring the thematic universe of the population - i.e. the issues, problems and contradictions which underlie people's everyday lives and which can form the material for their own education.[23] It is a process which is familiar to most community workers, and some educators, although often their employing bodies have difficulty in understanding it because they can see no 'concrete' results!

During this exploratory period the tutor/organiser met many of the teachers and parents in the various E.P.A. schools. He also became involved in a number of community activities, mainly concerned with housing problems and the lack of adequate social, youth and recreational facilities in the area. It soon became obvious that the people in the area suffered from a multitude of problems as a result of poverty, unemployment, redevelopment and overcrowding. It was also obvious that the parents were interested in their children's education but that their most pressing problems were outside the school. As a result there were numerous tenants associations and community groups involved in tackling the problems of housing, vandalism, poverty, unemployment and the general lack of recreational and social facilities.

It was also clear that terms such as 'educationally disadvantaged', 'deprived' had overtones of personal inadequacy and a culture of poverty which was totally at odds with the real situation. The people concerned were brave, resilient and resourceful in the face of tremendous problems not of their making. They were working class people deprived of resources, choice and power. Unlike Freire's 'investigators' it was not possible in this situation for the tutor/organiser to stand aside registering, as he suggests, everything in their notebooks! He became actively involved with local groups in these various activities providing resources and attempting to meet educational needs and interests on a number of fronts, using a variety of learning techniques from the informal to the formal. Thus he acted as a resource person or facilitator for various community groups involved in practical activities like setting up a community centre, providing a summer play scheme, organising a housing action scheme,

31

undertaking a survey of educational facilities in the area. On occasions this led to requests for more formal educational exercises in which residents spent more time analysing the causes of the problems they faced or learning skills to tackle them. Involvement in the practical work provided the tutor/organiser with the experience of real problems and issues which he was then able to use as learning material for the more formal educational exercises.

Other educational activities were more closely related not to aspects of community action, but to the problems arising from changing social and moral attitudes and values which closely affected family life in the various communities in the E.P.A. These took the form of group discussions, often with women, using their lives as the basis for discussion about the forces responsible for creating the common problems they all shared. The sessions were very informal and took place in pubs, clubs, community centres, and people's homes using a variety of educational resources (e.g. films, tapes, novels, T.V., local radio) which reflected back to people many of the problems they were facing.

Finally a variety of liberal, vocational and recreational courses were organised in similar informal surroundings, e.g. keep-fit, hairdressing, art, local history, 'O' levels. A range of educational institutions and organisations, e.g. the W.E.A., the University Extra-Mural Department, Evening Institutes, were involved in bringing their resources and personnel into the community. Local residents were also employed, and paid, as tutors to pass on their skills and knowledge to other residents on such topics as social security provision.

The schools did not play a central role in this process. However a number were used as centres for some of the educational activities outlined above. This often led to better communication and understanding between teachers and parents. However, most of the activities were held in community centres, pubs, church halls, homes, etc. They ranged over a wide spectrum of interests and needs and resulted in a broad range of activities, from learning through action to more traditional classes and courses, reflecting the heterogeneous nature of local needs and interests. This underlined the fact that it was not simply a matter of organising 'informal' adult education for the 'disadvantaged' but providing for a wide range of needs and abilities similar to those found in any community, middle class or working class, using a variety of methods and in a variety of settings from the informal to the formal.

Thus, the E.P.A. project demonstrated that the culture and environment of working class communities could be the basis, the starting-off point, for an examination of the problems of family and community life, providing the common sense knowledge and materials for popular education. It also demonstrated that a comprehensive community education service for working class communities was possible. People in priority areas (like people everywhere) had a wide range of interests, needs and abilities which adult education has failed to meet or utilise. Positive discrimination, flexibility, imagination, co-ordination and participation on the part of those involved (people and institutions) were essential in such a service. The problem lay with the providers, not the community.

The E.P.A. project was heavily influenced by the work of Freire and Bernstein on language and culture and Illich's network theory. Although successful in many respects it lacked a clear analysis of the problems facing the communities in inner Liverpool which located them within a wider social, economic and political context. It placed too much stress on the extent to which those problems could be resolved simply by co-ordinating services, and extending public participation in local affairs. It spread a very wide net which, although successful in terms of adult involvement, was limited in terms of its contribution to collective community action. Its approach was essentially liberal with an emphasis on the need for democratic local control of a comprehensive community adult education service in working class communities.

The Vauxhall Project

The Vauxhall project in the Scotland Road Area of Liverpool took place during the same period as the E.P.A. project and faced the same range of local problems. However its origins were located in the pioneering work of Keith Jackson at the Liverpool University Institute of Extension Studies which preceded and influenced both projects.[24]

Initially, in the late sixties, he had high hopes for community development as a means of reaching the broad bulk of the working class with relevant education and involving them with other organisations, institutions and government agencies, in seeking solutions to inner city problems. It was an approach very much in line with the comment from the Gulbenkian Report quoted above. In pursuit of this community development objective an attempt was made to provide a comprehensive 'vertical' community education service. 'Community development offers new situations with possibilities for adult education and research and also suggests ways in which adult education may develop as a more effective part of the total educational service, particularly in working class areas of large cities'.[25]

This service took a number of forms involving a range of professionals, community workers and local working class groups and leaders. Thus courses and seminars were provided for professional groups concerned with change and innovation particularly in regard to their relationships with working class communities in the inner city areas. These included clergy, social workers, police officers, administrators of social services. Similar courses and seminars were provided for professional community workers. Finally a range of educational services and resources were provided for local community groups and working class leaders. Regarding the latter the emphasis was on learning through doing and informal educational methods with the tutor filling a number of roles. 'Learning will take place through writing letters, organising petitions and surveys, meeting councillors and arranging social and other activities as well as through group discussion'.[26] However it was also recognised that requests for more formal education would arise particularly as groups become more formal and organised. A parallel was drawn between industrial relations courses for trade unionists and 'urban relations' for community groups and leaders.

However, just as the adult education work with the E.P.A. project moved away from the concept of the 'community school' to a more active involvement with local residents so, in the early seventies, when the Institute team became involved with the Home Office sponsored Vauxhall Community Development Project, it increasingly began to question the philosophy and strategy underlying the whole 'community' approach. The educational team from the Institute took a more critical view of the government sponsored community development strategy, offering instead an alternative theoretical framework and a more explicitly socialist set of values and objectives. 'In our own project we have seen no alternative but to see local people as part of the working class, exploited more than many in their social, economic and cultural environment in the centre of a large city whose economy is shaky and uncertain in Britain's present stage of development. This determines the educational structures we must encourage, emphasising wider contacts rather than local parochialism and the debate we think should the place around local social action. It is clear that this position creates difficulties when operating in the context of community development. 'Solidarity with working class activists' sets unhappily with 'non-directive approach offered to autonomous community groups'.'[27]

Arising from this position the Institute team consciously sought opportunities to engage local people in hard social analysis which attempted to link local issues and problems within a wider social economic and political context. They rejected the notion of 'informal' community education. Whilst accepting that a certain amount of learning did take place through active involvement in tackling local issues and problems the team stressed that many of those involved needed, and were capable of undertaking, academic-type work, but work bedded in the practical class issues affecting local people. This was a reaction to what they regarded as the woolliness of much community education and its concentration on the informal - cultural - language - local environment, aspect of education for the working class.

One such opportunity arose in the summer of 1972 with the Housing Finance Act. This was regarded as a highly relevant local and national issue. In dealing with it the team felt that local residents were entitled to educational resources even though 'a community development strategy might define it as irrelevant, external and political'.[28] They decided, in response to pressure from local residents, to offer a radical critique of the Act at a mass meeting and to link this to proposals for further analysis and practical action. However in the leaflets advertising the public meeting no mention was made of the two adult education organisations involved (the W.E.A. and the Institute) because, 'the theoretical position we have adopted requires a definite rejection of 'educational imperialism' in favour of an attempt to create working class control of the operation. We should prefer to be considered as educational advisors and consultants and for people not to feel obliged to adopt our institutionalised form'.[29] Over two hundred people attended the meeting to listen to a detailed critique of the Act, which made no concessions to a 'popular' approach in presenting the material. As a result seven smaller groups were addressed on this issue and one group eventually became an organised class on social theory and social problems.

Throughout the literature on this project, there is in fact a constant emphasis on the need to engage the residents in relevant education of a high standard, making few concessions to what was regarded as second class informal community discussion methods or learning through doing exercises. Working class activists were 'to be given the chance to come to terms with a subject, skill or field of knowledge so that they can understand its internal rules and become an expert as far as possible'.[30] This was regarded as the essential educational contribution to social action. Educators were to unite with the working class in fighting local issues but they were not to confuse this with their specific educational contribution to such action. However the team did become involved in the provision of other, less radical, education in the area. Under the title of 'Time off in Scotland Road', a range of courses and classes were organised, based primarily on discussions with activists in tenants associations and other local groups. Two secondary and one junior school offered their premises and resources, and classes were provided in boat building, metal work and mechanics, home maintenance, woodwork, cookery, talking about books, swimming, art and design, local history, Spanish, city problems. Other classes, more explicitly linked to social action in the area, e.g. housing, finance, vandalism, unemployment, etc., were also provided. These were all continuous learning sessions, distinct, but not separate, from on-going social action.

As a result of this work and the lessons arising out of it, a 'Second Chance to Learn Project' was initiated in 1976 with working class students from all over the city studying full-time on day release, over a period of 20 weeks. However, paradoxically there is some evidence that this is creaming off bright working class leaders who regard it as a means of individual, not collective, development. 'Second Chance has always had to come to terms with the tension between the interests of the politically committed who form a coherent and vocal minority of the students and the needs of the minimally class-conscious students. We have recognised the advantages for both types of student and for tutors from this mix, but we also hold that adult education for the working class has to offer stimulus to both the committed and the uncommitted'.[31]

Obviously this conflict has created tensions and problems. The solution offered is, in some respects, a return to a more broadly based community education programe. 'It may be possible to avoid the creaming off of activists if priority is given to the development of forms of education closely tied to the needs of the community. This is not to deny the right of students to expect support in their efforts to reach university. On the other hand, the vast majority who don't make the break with work or community have at least an equal right to forms of education which advance their struggles and interests'.[32] In an effort to create such opportunties, a Liverpool Inner Areas Adult

35

Education Consortium was formed in 1978 to provide a popular educational network linking education in local communities with the day release Second Chance Scheme and a new adult residential college, the Northern College, in Barnsley, Yorkshire. This was in some respects a return to the comprehensive community adult education programme developed by the E.P.A. Project. 'The under-lying logic of the Consortium's composition is that it aims to serve three functions for those sections of the population who are worst served by present educational provision. Schemes such as Home Link and Vauxhall provide initial access to adult education, through strong local links, sensitivity to local needs and concerns, and a programme of basic education, although not exclusively that (Vauxhall and Charles Woolton for example, both have schemes for students interested in G.C.E.'s and higher education). Second Chance particularly, but not exclusively, gives access to more advanced study and prepares students for mature entrance to higher education. Finally the Northern College, with Partnership finance, undertakes to provide places for a number of students from Liverpool'.[33]

Community Education Models
Although each of the projects discussed above had its own distinct philosophy they both illustrate the variety of approaches to be found in many community education initiatives. They also illustrate the tensions and contradictions to be found in such projects, particularly between the individualist and collective approach to education and social change. All of these approaches are, however, to some degree departures from everyday practice and thus, relatively speaking, radical. However it is possible to discern, amongst the mixture of approaches, a number of different models which reflect not only different educational pedagogies but different views of the world and the role of education in the process of social and political change.

(1) A Community Organisation/Education Model
The first model is one which attempts to combine aspects of community 'organisation' and community 'work' and relate these to adult education provision. This entails concentrating on the effective co-ordination and delivery of the wide variety of educational re-sources available to meet local needs and interests. It usually implies appointing out-reach workers - community education tutors - to work outside institutions in local communities where there is little or no take up of adult education provision, thus linking the community to the latter. This, in itself, is nothing new. It is the traditional W.E.A. tutor organiser role, and it has been successfully adopted by some community schools and Colleges of Further Education. It differs however in a number of respects: (i) the concentration on specific working class communities; (ii) the attempt to provide not only for working class participation but control of the programme; (iii) the comprehensive nature of the resources now available for adult education and the extent to which these can be co-ordinated in an educational 'network' and related to local needs.

Both the E.P.A. and Vauxhall Projects used this model in aspects of their work, especially for the provision of recreational and vocational courses. Some initiatives using this model have placed great stress on the need for informal educational methods and techniques.[34] Others have succeeded in providing traditional formal courses and classes within an informal 'organisational structure'.[35] Usually it is a mixture of both. In fact, as the E.P.A. and Vauxhall projects discovered the education which is often demanded, the education which initially appears most effectively to meet local articulated needs is often very traditional, very instrumental. Thus the success is providing courses and classes in 'O' levels, car maintenance, hairdressing, etc. This is both understandable and realistic given people's experience of education and their knowledge of what it is for, and about. It appears that once the formal structure of adult education is removed many working class adults are eager and willing to participate in traditional adult education 'fare'. This community education model is, in fact, an extension of the liberal tradition, bringing education to the people in their own surroundings and on their own terms. It differs in the attempt to break down the distinctions between different forms of provision, i.e., liberal recreational, vocational and to co-ordinate and make openly available the great variety of adult education resources and opportunities. The relationship between this 'community education service' and social change is seen in terms of the contribution those who participate in this more flexible adult education service can, or will, make to their own development and that of their community.

The major criticism of this model (echoing the Council of Europe report referred to in chapter one)[36] is that, although it can be very successful in encouraging working class adults to participate in education, encouraging personal development, and possibly providing a ladder out of 'deprived' communities, it leaves the position of the general community unresolved. It does nothing for problems of poverty and inequality which community development strategies seek to eliminate. That is the contradiction the Vauxhall Project sought to resolve.

(2) A Community Development/Education Model

The second model is one which attempts to meet this criticism by concentrating on a mixture of community work and community development. Adult educators operate like Schon's 'marginal men',[37] working in local communities in a variety of community projects providing information, resources, advice and, when the occasion arises, opportunities for more systematic learning and training in specific skills and techniques relevant to such action. In this community development model an effort is also made to educate the institutions and organisations concerned with the provision of services and resources for the local community. They are provided with a 'community' dimension in their training and education i.e. how 'they' see 'us'. Thus courses are provided for local councillors, clergy, police, planners, social workers, etc., as well as profesional community workers and local working class leaders.

The early work at the Liverpool Institute of Extension Studies

was important in developing this model, in which community development and community education were viewed as processes which could
involve the whole community in a concerted effort to resolve local
problems.[38] It is an extension of the liberal/reform tradition, one
more actively involved in local affairs working closely with community
groups and institutions. It accepts the nature of the pluralist society
and concentrates on improving communication and understanding
between the various conflicting groups in an effort to improve local
community problems. It is a model which owes a lot to that early
Gulbenkian report.

The major weakness in this approach is its assumption that the
problems found in deprived areas can be resolved by such co-
operation, co-ordination and improved understanding at local level.
As many of the Home Office sponsored Community Development
Projects in the 70's soon realised, this view rests on certain naive
assumptions about the nature of poverty and deprivation. 'The
usefulness to the state of defining the urban problem to the residents
of the older industrial areas as a sickness to be 'treated' hardly needs
stressing. It fits neatly alongside the idea that it is a marginal
problem to be solved by increased discussion . . . . . The emphasis on
'tackling social needs' in isolation inevitably distracts attention from
the root causes of the problem by focussing attention upon personal
deficiencies. The people themselves are to blame for the problems
caused by capital'.[39]

(3) A Community Action/Education Model

The third model places greater stress on combining community
education and community *action*, on the role of conflict in resolving
local problems and the importance of creating alternative institutions
and organisations. It emphasises the need for adult educators to
identify with, and commit themselves to, local working class
communities and the groups and organisations found in such
communities. There is a strong belief that community action is in
itself an educational process one which, in line with Freire's pedagogy,
offers opportunities for consciousness raising about those wider
arrangements in society which cause local problems. 'It would be our
contention that, in this process of trying to change the situation they
find themselves in, residents come to a deeper understanding of the
factors which affect their lives and realise more clearly the need for
co-ordinated efforts with other organised groups to achieve any
significant shift of resources towards themselves. Initially the
concern is with 'information for use in preparing plans'. Later it is a
concern with 'resources' of capital and labour and their 'control' and
management'.[40]

Thus, although there are attempts to provide instrumental
education for those engaged in community action the stress is also on
radical political education. In terms of educational methods this
implies dialogue and discussion, linked not only to community action
and the wider political system, but to personal life, i.e., the problems,
tensions and opportunities brought about by changes in social attitudes
and values particularly, as Ralph Miliband stresses, 'the demand for

38

more democratic relations in daily life, between man and woman in the home, between parents and children in schools, in all spheres where people come together by necessity or choice. This is a tremendous business which undermines strongly held attitudes and deeply ingrained customs and modes of behaviour and which presents a manifold and diffuse and still unfocussed challenge to class-ridden and class-encrusted society such as this. The 'cultural' revolution which this signifies is now well under way'.[41]

In educational terms there is thus more concern with 'culture' in its widest sense and for educators to be seen as cultural workers, linking traditional politics to the politics of everyday personal life, through movements like the feminists. Community art, community media, community publishing ventures provide the imaginative material created by people for their own education.[42]

In this model the concept of 'community' is also taken seriously as a base for action and education, particularly in terms of the opportunities it affords for helping people to create, or recreate, alternative institutions at local level which offer them an opportunity to care for, and about, each other and to control vital aspects of their everyday lives. It attempts to link the 'cultural' revolution with a new sense of community in which the desire for freedom and solidarity can be combined within new local institutional arrangements. 'There is a profound spontaneous desire for what we might call organic community amongst people of all classes in Britain. The word community is popular because through it people can express this yearning for social wholeness, a mutuality and interrelatedness as opposed to alienated, fragmented, antagonistic social world of daily experience. Linked with this deisre for warm relatedness is a deisre for stability'.[43]

This model has been criticised for its stress on local alternatives rather than broad social movements as solutions to the problems of inequality; its tendency to regard everything in which an adult educator is involved as 'educational'; its lack of intellectual content, offering people instead a second class 'informal' education which underestimates their ability to undertake more sustained study; its emphasis on 'process' rather than content and motivation. Its supporters are aware of the need to think in a more systematic way about the educational aspects of community action, particularly in the domestic sphere. However it would appear that this sort of work has not developed as well as it should. Nevertheless, it is possible to discern in this model links with that earlier 19th century radical educational tradition discussed in chapter one, and the work of Highlander and Antigonish.

(4) A Social Action/Education Model

The fourth and final model, the one closely identified with the later work of the Liverpool Institute of Extension Studies in the Vauxhall project, has more in common with the Labour College Movement in the U.S.A. and Great Britain. It places greater stress on motivation and content; on hard educational effort; on social, rather than community, action; on 'working class' rather than 'community'

against Freirean principles ?? cf Introduction

education. It is suspicious of the view that community action is, in itself, a learning process, or that just because an educator is involved in providing support and assistance for a particular local initiative it is an educational process. Education must be more structured and systematic. Educators must however act in solidarity with local people, aligning themselves with local community action, seeking to provide specific forms of educational support which illuminate the problems which local people seek to resolve.

There is more stress on locating, through education, the origins of local community problems in the larger social, economic and political structures in society. This is to be done not through informal dialogue and discussion but by strengthening motivation so that working class adults are prepared to undertake such hard intellectual effort. Workers must be convinced of their ability to undertake what is, to many of them, a daunting educational 'journey', by boosting their confidence and self image. This is a model which reaffirms certain aspects of the liberal tradition found in the trade union education work pioneered by some University Extra-Mural Departments; i.e., hard sustained intellectual study in which workers are given the best that is available and treated as adults who are willing, and capable, of undertaking work of a university level. It differs in its rejection of an 'objective' stance by the tutors concerned, and its more open commitment to and links with radical social action. However this does not imply, as in the Labour College tradition, a rigid dogmatic approach to education. It is much more open and critical, less concerned to 'convert' than educate, a combination of the best in Highlander, the W.E.A. and the Labour College traditions.

However, it has been criticised for its narrow interpretation of education and the possible dangers of creating an educational elite. 'Courses on the political economy of cities are fine, but very few community activists are at the point where such phrases mean anything to them. Such courses are more often run for the benefit of left-professionals (including community workers) with perhaps a couple of token working class activists or trade unionists'.[44]

Conclusions

The last comment is a little pessimistic about the possibilities of engaging community activists in hard sustained education as the Second Chance to Learn Project in Liverpool has proven. However, that initiative faced certain contradictions indicated above, i.e., that it is too narrow and can be used as a 'ladder' out of the community. It appears that in their admirable decision to prove that many working class adults are capable of undertaking, and benefitting from, this sort of education they have over-reacted to other forms of education linked to community action. The radical critique associated with the Vauxhall project and the educational forms arising from it - whilst important - are unnecessarily limited in scope and do less than justice to the complexity and variety of community action and the educational responses necessary to meet the latter.

The last decade in Northern Ireland has, contrary to the picture presented in the media, seen such a great variety of initiatives in community action and education. This experience is of more than purely local interest. Northern Ireland is *not* a unique situation, some strange and irrelevant phenomenon beyond the pale. It is, in many respects, an extreme manifestation of processes at work in other western societies - particularly those discussed in the previous chapter.

Thus the communal conflict and the extreme social and economic deprivation found here give added relevance and significance to the debate about the nature of community action as a force for social change, and about the relationship between the latter and community education. In particular the experience in Northern Ireland helps to illuminate and clarify the weaknesses and strengths of the various 'models' of community education discussed in this chapter. It is the purpose of the rest of this book to discuss and analyse that experience and to draw some general conclusions regarding the role of adult education in social change and more specifically, the relationship between community education and community action.

Before doing so however it is necessary to say something about the role of community action in Northern Ireland over the last decade.

NOTES

1. See, for example: K. Jackson, 'Adult Education and Community Development' in *Studies in Adult Education*, Vol. 2, No. 2, October, 1970; J. Harrison, 'Community Work and Adult Education' in *Studies in Adult Education*, Vol. 6, No. 1, April, 1974; K.H. Lawson, 'Community Education - a critical assessment' *Adult Education*, Vol. 50, No. 1, May, 1977; C. Fletcher and N. Thompson, *Issues in Community Education* (Falmer Press, 1980).

2. R. Shaw, 'Adult Education and the Working Class', in *Studies in Adult Education*, Vol. 2, No. 1, 1970.

3. Workers' Educational Association *Unfinished Business: W.E.A. Policy Statement*, (W.E.A. London, 1969).

4. T. Lovett, 'Community Adult Education'. *Studies in Adult Education*, Vol. 3, No. 1, 1971.

5. B. Bernstein, (i) *Class, Codes and Control. Vols. 1 and 2.* (Routledge and Kegan Paul, London, 1971), (ii) 'A Critique of the Concept of Compensatory Education, in *Education for Democracy* Eds. D. Rubenstein and C. Stoneman (Penguin, Harmondsworth, 1970).

6. P. Freire, *Cultural Action for Freedom.* (Penguin, Harmondsworth, 1972).

7. I. Illich, *De-schooling Society.* (Calder and Boyars, London, 1972).

8. P. Marris and M. Rein, *Dilemmas of Social Reform.* (Routledge and Kegan Paul, London, 1972).

9. G. Smith and T. Smith, 'The Community School - a base for community development' in *Community Work One.* Eds. D. Jones and M. Mayo (Routledge and Kegan Paul, London, 1974).

10. Calouste Gulbenkian Foundation *Community Work and Social Change - A Report on Training.* (Longman, London, 1968).

11. W.W. Biddle and L.J. Biddle, *The Community Development*

Process. (Holt, Rinehart and Winston, London, 1966), p. 243.

12. B. Groombridge, 'The Wincham Experiment'. *Studies in Adult Education.* Vol. 8, No. 2, October, 1976.

13. M.P. Follett, *The New State.* (1918).

14. B. Groombridge, op. cit., p. 123.

15. Fletcher and Thompson, op. cit.

16. T. Lovett, *Adult Education, Community Development and the Working Class.* (Ward Lock Educational, London, 1975).

17. K. Jackson, op. cit., and K. Jackson and B. Ashcroft, 'Adult Education and Social Action', in *Community Work One*, Eds. D. Jones and M. Mayo, (Routledge and Kegan Paul, London, 1971).

18. A.H. Halsey, (ed.) *Educational Priority, Vol. 1, E.P.A. Problems and Policies.* (H.M.S.O., 1972).

19. E. Midwinter, *Priority Education.* (Penguin, Harmondsworth, 1972).

20. Central Advisory Council For Education, *Half our Future.* (H.M.S.O., 1963).

21. Central Advisory Council For Education, *Children and their Primary Schools.* (H.M.S.O., 1967).

22. T. Lovett, *Adult Education Community Development and the Working Class.* op. cit.

23. P. Freire, *Pedagogy of the Oppressed*, Chapter III, (Penguin, Harmondsworth, 1972).

24. K. Jackson, op. cit.

25. Ibid., p. 156.

26. Ibid., p. 169.

27. K. Jackson, 'The Marginality of Community Development', in *International Review of Community Development*, 1973, p. 38.

28. Ashcroft and Jackson, op. cit., p. 55.

29. Ibid., p. 57.

30. The Marginality of Community Development, p. 27, op. cit.

31. M. Yarnit, 'Second Chance to Learn, Liverpool. Class and Adult Education', in *Adult Education for a Change*, Ed. J.L. Thompson (Hutchinson and Co., Ltd., London, 1980), p. 190.

32. Ibid., p. 130.

33. Ibid., p. 188.

34. P. Fordham, G. Poulton and L. Randle, *Learning Networks in Adult Education.* (Routledge and Kegan Paul, London, 1979).

35. See, for example: C.S. McConnell, (ed.), *The People's Classroom - a Scottish Case Study on Community Controlled Adult Education*, (James Watt Collge, Greenock, 1980); M. Newman, *The Poor Cousin: A Study of Adult Education*, (Allen and Unwin, 1979); D. Rowlands, S. Griffiths, F. Gaffakin, and D. Ray, *The Community Education Project.* (Queen's University, Belfast, 1979).

36. *Permanent Education - Evaluation of Pilot Experiments - Interim Report.* Council for Cultural Co-operation, Steering Committee on Permanent Education. (Council of Europe, Strasbourg, 1974).

37. D. Schon, *Beyond the Stable State.* (Temple Smith, London, 1971).

38. Jackson, op. cit.

39. *Gilding the Ghetto - The State and the Poverty Experiments*, Community Development Projects (Inter Project Editorial Team 1977), p. 55.

40. A. Simpson and W. Williams, 'Community Education and Community Action, in *Issues in Community Education*, op. cit. p. 76.

41. R. Miliband, 'The Future of Socialism in England', *Socialist Register, 1977*, (Merlin Press, London, 1977) p. 42.

42. S. Westwood, 'Adult Education and the Sociology of Education - An Exploration' in *Adult Education for a Change*, op. cit.

43. C. Kirkwood, 'Adult Education and the Concept of Community', in *Adult Education*, Vol. 51, No. 3, 1978, pp. 148-149.

44. J. Smith, 'Hard Lines and Soft Options in Community Work', in *Political Issues and Community Work*, Ed. Paul Curno, (Routledge and Kegan Paul, London, 1978), p. 28.

Chapter 4

SOCIAL CHANGE AND COMMUNITY ACTION
IN NORTHERN IRELAND

A Society under Siege

It has been said in recent years that Northern Ireland has a problem for every solution. Over the last decade many of these problems have received considerable attention from the world media. The spotlight, however, has rarely strayed from the political violence colloquially known as 'The Troubles'. Outside attitudes have fluctuated from amused tolerance of an anachronistic 'war of religion' to virulent condemnations of the bloody Irish; and from liberal platitudes about the need for 'love' to a romantic idealism of 'the Revolution'. Apart from passing reference to high rates of unemployment and the grinding poverty extensively experienced throughout the Province, little attention is given to issues that affect the quality of life in working-class areas. The best known communities are those that have gained greatest political notoriety - The Bogside, the Shankill Road, Bally-murphy, Sandy Row, etc. Even recent re-examinations of Irish history have tended to concentrate on a version of events that virtually ignores the development of social action and specifically of the Labour Movement in Northern Ireland.

While it is not possible to undertake an honest analysis of community action without acknowledging the fact that there is a war being waged in the Province, it is equally misleading to exaggerate the impact of the latter. In terms of the working-class, the aims of the combatants are limited. The importance ascribed to the constitutional destiny of Northern Ireland means that the class struggle and the women's struggle tend to be relegated to the side-lines. The community struggle for greater local democracy and an improved quality of life varies between being seen as a useful tactic or as a red-herring - distracting attention from 'the real' struggle.

It is ironic, that while the uninitiated visitor may well interpret the rubble-covered inner city areas of Belfast as being the victim of bombs, it is more likely that they are suffering the side effects of redevelopment. Indeed, while it is true that wall slogans and fortified pubs are constant reminders of 'The Troubles', as likely as not, that now famous West Belfast Slogan 'Is there life before death?' was inspired by the daily struggle for survival in a deprived community.

The reality of this deprivation can be seen in the range of

problems confronting one community worker in the Creggan Estate in Derry:-

> Well I think of all the social problems there are. I mean Creggan has got everything. It's got poor housing. It's got people who are on low income - those that are employed are on low incomes. Those that are unemployed are the majority. When you're talking in terms of Creggan - widows, pensioners, single parent families, you name it we've got it. We've got poor facilities medically, we've got poor facilities in so far as shopping is concerned, telephones .... even for somewhere to post your letter .... we just seem to be deprived. I sometimes think that if we were back in the biblical days and John the Baptist were running around looking for a wilderness, he wouldn't go to the desert, he would come to Creggan ....

It is true that Creggan is a particularly deprived ghetto community, with some 50% male unemployment, but there are few community activists who would be unable to identify with the issues raised. Even the problems directly related to Creggan's notorious political reputation are not - if police are substituted for the army and R.U.C. - without parallel for many young blacks and Asians in inner-city communities throughout Britain. As is pointed out by the same community worker:-

> .... and the youth of Creggan in particular, it's incredible, particularly over the last ten years with all the violence and the troubles that here have been. Young persons between the ages of 14 to 24 or 25, can't walk on the streets after dark because he's getting picked up, he's getting harrassed by the British Army, he's afraid to go anywhere unless he's with two or three other fellows, because there's a certain amount of safety in numbers. You know he can't come to the Youth Centre a lot of the time because there is a certain rotation and unless he happens to be a club member he won't come in. He can't go to the pub because he's too young, so I mean where does he go? .... Sit in the house all day or all night .... it's ridiculous, it's shameful ....

Given the bitterness generated by over a decade of such experience, the intensity of feeling in communities in Northern Ireland, may well be greater than their working-class counterparts in Liverpool or Dublin. However, there is a shared concern about the range of community issues that have been identified in these indignant contributions - poor facilities, lack of social amenities, low pay, unemployment, poverty, lack of provision for youth, etc. The difference in Northern Ireland is the scale and concentration of these problems and the fact that popular attention is more often focussed on the 'National Question' and, consequently, the long term aspiration of community groups is constantly under question. The Northern experience also differs in that community action has not become a haven for 'disillusioned politics' - but rather has become an arena for political debate.

THE ISSUES - AS PEOPLE SEE THEM

Given that community action has represented an attempt 'to confront the dual problems of necessity and desire', the pressure to satisfy necessity is so great in Northern Ireland that it is somewhat amazing that aspiration and desire have managed to survive! However, the long-term nature of necessity in the Province has resulted in resourceful, creative and enduring initiatives in working class communities. The recognition of this development cannot shadow or excuse the fact that the working class have suffered appalling deprivation. Aspects of the latter are described below by individuals from a range of communities on both sides of the sectarian divide. Irrespective of their varying political perspectives, the issues that they raise are class issues - although they may not always be commonly perceived as such.

1.   **Poverty**
     .... the girls get free dinners in school. Their tickets are a different colour from the paying children. That also leaves the children with a mark against them. You just cannot make Supplementary go round no matter what you do. You don't get out. There's no social life. I get £36 a week. I am paying £9 for rent and when I do that and pay my electric .... and pay the coal and everything else, I am just left with nothing. Some mornings my children just walk to school, I haven't even got the bus money. It's just as simple as that, you have nothing and nobody cares ....

Since this Newry woman spoke about her predicament (in 1979) her overall position has got worse - there have been constant rent increases and increasingly rigid social security legislation. The same applies in this Derry case:-

Well I'm a widow and I have got eight children - as a matter of fact I have nine, but one's in Long Kesh - and I'm living on £41-90 a week. We had a rise there last year .... they gave it to us in the family allowance to take it off the pension. I tried for Supplementary for clothes for the young lads, because I have two sons and they're unemployed, the rest are all at school. I applied for free meals and I was turned down. The man came up and I asked why I was turned down, he said I was drawing £5 over the limit. My house also was so damp that .... I got in central heating and it's costing me a bomb, and right now I can't afford to turn it on. Things are so bad now that I have to go out and work and leave the family to try and make up a wage for to try and buy food and clothes and one thing and another.

In the existing economic climate - pariticularly in areas such as

Derry - this woman would be very fortunate if she was able to get a job. She could also be considered relatively lucky coming from a closely knit community in which a friend or relative might look after her children. Throughout the whole of Northern Ireland there are some five day-care centres for children under five, with the majority of these being attached to academic institutions or work places.

The cases cited above are not exceptions, nor are they confined to one section of the community. A range of welfare rights studies and surveys confirms that Northern Ireland is the most deprived region of the United Kingdom. Indeed it merits consideration as one of the poorest regions of Western Europe. The statistics are as depressing as the individual cases themselves - with little hope of improvement on either front.

2. Unemployment

Figures for unemployment are equally grim - and again show little prospect of change for the better. Northern Ireland has suffered from high rates of unemployment for generations, but between June 1973 and June 1979 the overall unemployment rate for the Province doubled. By 1979 there was 10.3% unemployed in the Province as against 5.6% throughout Great Britian. In one town, Newry, there was 264 registered unemployed per registered unfilled vacancy that same year.

There was, and are, concentrations of unemployment and poverty in certain areas. A government study of Ballymurphy (in West Belfast) showed that by 1978 there was some 48.7% unemployed, economically active heads of households; 51% of heads of households with income lower than £40 per week and 95% of heads of households earning less than £75 per week.[1] In a slightly broader context West Belfast has 33% of the city's population and only some 17% of job opportunities. This has become particularly relevant since the outbreak of 'The Troubles' as the resulting ghettoisation makes many unwilling to travel to work outside their own areas for fear of sectarian attacks.

In more concrete terms a number of unemployed people described their frustration and sense of hopelessness:-

(a) It's ten years since I've been employed. Last time I was in England working. It's about fifteen years since I worked in Derry itself. My opinion of being on the dole, it wrecks your confidence. The first couple of months you're alright, but after that you start - you don't give a damn, you don't care like how you go on like, you know. You start to lie in bed later and everything. You couldn't care less about anything. I think it destroys your personality after a while. Because for myself anyway, years ago I was free from worry, free, happy-go-lucky like. But now I'm a sort of cynical person . . . .

(b) . . . . it sort of wrecks the home life too like you know, I have two young lads working, and you're getting them up in the morning. You're trying to throw them out of bed after six and they're looking at you and growling - wondering you aren't making an effort yourself to go out, you know. And as I was saying earlier like, you're about the house all day, because you can't afford to go out. The wife's getting fed up looking at you hanging about . . . . I think it wrecks your life completely . . . .

Widespread poverty is inextricably linked to low pay in Northern Ireland. Again, pay levels in the Province, particularly for male workers, are lower than those prevailing in the rest of the United Kingdom.

Equally, and for many of the same reasons, it is alleged that many industries are not noted for good working conditions. This, in turn, has inevitable repercussions on both individuals and families in working class communities:-

. . . . what we have at the moment is no choice. Now there may be vacancies in a place so why don't the unemployed take up this offer? But shift work is a very, very bad kind of routine for anyone to work in for any length of time . . . . a lot of people have had their health broken. It's not really a very healthy place to work . . . .

The point made by this Craigavon activist was supported by a local man:-

. . . . I worked for ten years. I have now been out of it two years this coming Christmas, and I'm out with a complaint that I got which is a chest complaint, and it has left me now that I can't go anywhere for a job, for I won't get one . . . .

This man is one of many that make up the high number of disability claimants in Northern Ireland like so many others, he is the victim of a depressed economy - the latter being characterised by the attendant ills of unemployment, low pay and poor conditions.

3. Lack of Facilities
The depressed state of many working class communities alongside a high rate of unemployment can herald other problems:-

. . . . the young unemployed, they're very frustrated because they cannot get a job. If they are offered a job, it's only maybe a labourer and they have to travel miles and miles for £10-£11 a week. And they turn this down. They won't even go to the interviews because they say it's not worth it. So the result is they're hanging around street corners. They get bored doing this, so then the next step is breaking and entering . . . . they are caught. The next thing is they're landed in court . . . .

This Newry youth worker attributed the fact that many un-employed youngsters got into trouble to the lack of adequate provision for them in the community.

More often than not complaints about the lack of amenities

occur in newly developed areas or in the large post-war housing estates. Creggan, in Derry, is an example of the latter. In cases of re-development of working class areas, not alone are facilities often not provided, but the old sense of community solidarity tends to be shattered. The main victims of this change are the elderly. One old lady from the Shankill Road area of Belfast explained:-

> People's afraid to go out at night. Do you see here, see after six o'clock you wouldn't see the face of nobody .... you have to keep your door shut ....

This is at odds with the close street and neighbourhood communities that used to exist in these areas.

It is indeed the elderly, the handicapped and the mothers of young children that tend to be most affected by the lack of adequate planning and the cut-backs engaged in by the authorities. They feel the effect of lack of shops, poor bus services and difficulty of access to phones. These vulnerable sections of the community are also the ones that are hit hardest by vandalism and the destruction of the few facilities that are provided. Thus a vicious circle is established that has rarely been effectively challenged. Frustration from unemployment and lack of available facilities results in general vandalism, which then provides the rationale for those who argue against the provision of facilities in deprived working class areas. The sum total is that proposed playgrounds take on the appearance of disorganised scrap heaps and steel-plated shops would do credit to Dodge City. The only light relief is provided by the wall artists - formal, community arts subsidised - and informal, private enterprise, alike.

The list of issues, grievances and very real problems that affect working class communities could continue at length. Comments about the cost of living, bad housing and poor repairs, lack of opportunities and the plight of single parent families are all equally valuable and are grounded in bitter experience. To merely list them however, would be to do an injustice to the incredible spirit and endurance of such communities. As one community worker pointed out:-

> .... this is an estate of two and a half thousand houses and there is something like a population of thirteen thousand .... Perhaps the authorities are fortunate that the people up here have a certain amount of self-respect for themselves. God knows how they managed to keep this about themselves with the situation being as it is. But somehow the people have managed to keep themselves together .... Maybe it's a pity that people haven't lost the head a bit more, that they haven't gone beserk and showed up the authorities for what they are, you know. Ask me what they are, I don't know - unfeeling, inhuman, unconcerned. That's the impression we get up here, that nobody cares, nobody's interested ....

This feeling of frustration was put somewhat more succinctly by an elderly resident on the Shankill Road:-

.... you don't get anywhere no matter how much you fight here. The Provos is fighting for political status for three or four years now and they've no chance of getting it back - so what chance has the Shankill got to get what they want?

Community Action - Baptism of Fire

Despite the lack of optimism about the odds for any improvement in conditions, Northern Ireland has been noted for its wide range of community initiatives. As in the past a certain element of desperation has helped to spur these enterprises - the 'up by your own boot straps' syndrome. In the sixties this philosophy inspired the development of the Credit Union movement and local Housing Aid societies. The 'No-Go' areas of the early seventies were to benefit from this experience. It is true, however, that such developments tended to be concentrated in Nationalist/Roman Catholic communities and were at a deeper level, an indication of alienation from a state which not alone did not deliver the goods but was also seen as sectarian.

Unlike Britain these early movements were not encouraged by Government policy, they were more likely to receive the patronage of the local Parish Priest and Nationalist Councillor. Consequently there was little conscious identification of working-class interests. The concept of 'community' tended to be interpreted in local, defensive and often sectarian terms.

The advent of 'The Troubles' did not help to challenge this situation at the neighbourhood level. Political necessity made use of the community action tactic to develop local vigilante forces. For those in less threatened societies organising community life behind barricades, mobilizing support for marches or arranging supplies during the 1974 Ulster Workers' Council strike may seem far removed from the average stock of community tactics. In Northern Ireland, however, the difference has often proved to be merely one of degree. Although the range of underlying political motivation varied, community activists and organisations tended to respond to the immediate needs of 'their' community. Even workers in the government-established Community Relations Commission periodically found that the pressure of the moment dictated their work. Indeed the immense practical help given by the Commission staff to the victims of intimidation in 1971 was described by the Commission Chairman as:-

.... in many ways .... our finest hour.

The Northern Ireland Community Relations Commission which met for the first time in December 1969 was an element in a packet of measures introduced by the Westminster Government. It was an attempt to apply the Community Development Project approach to a situation that was found basically incomprehensible. However, given the necessity to come to terms with sectarian attitudes, the Commision tended to adopt a 'human relations' emphasis and shied away from the class-based socio-economic analysis adopted by many of the Community Development Projects in Britain.

Through his direction of the Commission staff, and their work with local activists, the director of the C.R.C., Hywell Griffith, had a formative influence on community development, although the tensions experienced within the Commission itself, and the political pressures placed on it, were never to allow a uniform approach.[2] Maurice Hayes, the first Chairman of the Community Relations Commission, had however a very definite view of 'the problem':-

> Put crudely the struggle in Northern Ireland is about power, about who has it, who wants it and how it can be shared. Any approach to the problem of relationships between the communities, which ignores this reality is bound to be superficial.[3]

This intervention in 1972 queried the concept of 'reconciliation' as an adequate basis for community development. It was a controversy that was to continue over the years.

The debate around the issue of power raises, yet again, the ambiguity of community action and the difficulties in reconciling the long-term aspirations of those involved. On both sides of the sectarian divide in Northern Ireland the weaker sections of the working class have experienced a sense of powerlessness. In both cases it proved to be the 'seed bed of community action' carefully nurtured by local activists and Community Relations Staff; however, there were few who were prepared to confront the devisive question - 'power to do what?'

Work tended to continue around less politically controversial local issues. The growth of articulate, self-confident community groups was one of the most remarkable developments of the early years of 'The Troubles'. Community papers such as the 'Andersonstown News', 'Community Mirror', etc., were launched - as were co-operatives, local Action Groups and Redevelopment Associations. There was a tendency for such groups to be formed in areas most affected by paramilitary activities and problems of social deprivation. Local co-ordinating bodies were also established - such as the Greater West Belfast Community Association in 1973.

The Community Relations Commission provided a certain degree of support for many of these developments. It was itself, however, to fall victim of the short-lived 'power sharing' executive in 1974. Its demise was to signal a series of community conferences which debated, among other things, the possibility of co-ordinating community aciton in the Province. These conferences provided a range of community activists with the opportunity to indulge in not altogether comfortable reflection. A number of conclusions were reached:-

> The experience of the Greater West Belfast Community Association in the field of community action is at best a harrowing one, at worst a recipe for violence. Violence in this domain is neither the violence of nationalism nor the counter violence of fear. It is the violence of impotence, and the general point reiterated by

a number of the participant organisations is, we cannot opt out of our responsibilities.[4]

A political awareness of the context in which they worked produced, amongst the community representatives present, a mix of utopian demands and deep political disagreement - the latter often reflecting community allegiances. On the one hand it was agreed that:-

We must have community government designed to meet the needs and fullest participation of people in the community, not community needs and involvement subject to the design of government.[5]

However, the two resolutions calling for an end to 'internment without trial' resulted in voting - 45 in favour - 36 against and 19 abstentions.

One of the more realistic, if limited, levels of community co-ordination, a continuous round of committee meetings, seminars and conferences, finally produced C.O.N.I. - the Community Organisation of Northern Ireland - which accepted the aim of ensuring that:-

People achieve more control over the decisions which affect their own lives at every level . . . .[6]

This optimistic ambition was not to be achieved despite C.O.N.I.'s involvement in many community campaigns. Indeed, developments on the macro political stage were to result in an ever-greater distancing of decision making from local communities in Northern Ireland.

The community campaigns launched reflected the issues and problems that have already been referred to - problems of redevelopment, of poverty, of debt and issues relating to housing. The lack of success that often resulted produced a combination of experineced workers and disillusionment. As a result of this many felt that a change of tactic was necessary. This led to the establishment of a wide range of issue-oriented pressure groups, many of them linked to similar organisations and developments in Britain.

The other strain placed on attempts to co-ordinate community action throughout Northern Ireland was the fear of sectarian alignment. The Ulster Community Action Group had been set up and, like C.O.N.I., was largely funded by the Department of Education. U.C.A.G. was very clearly geared to work with loyalist (Protestant) communities and to co-ordinate and promote initiatives in these areas. It is true that it tended to confine its activities to the Greater Belfast area and the north-east of the Province, and did not engage in community campaigns to the same extent as C.O.N.I. Yet its existence reflected the fragmentation of community action and the impossibility of ignoring the political tensions. By 1980/81 both C.O.N.I. and U.C.A.G. had virtually disbanded - the former in a formal manner, the latter in all but name. The reasons for their disappearance from the community scene reflected the increasing sense of powerlessness as well as a feeling that the situation demanded a new approach. That approach was to result in the pressure group era.

Pressure - for Education and Change
The establishment of pressure groups reflected the growth of social movements and the limitations of localised community action. The Women's Movement - which was a relatively new phenomenon in Northern Ireland - gave rise to a range of single issue groups. The plight of single parent families - battered women and their children; women dependent on welfare benefits; were all raised and discussed within the overall position of women in Irish society. A crop of voluntary organisations publicised issues that the community movement had hitherto tended to overlook. They combined a campaigning role, with the provision of services and facilities, besides undertaking a general educative function. A new respect could be perceived for research and expertise that had often been discounted by community activists - consequently such organisations were acknowledged as being able to speak with insight on their own selected area of interest and concern. Nevertheless, a balance had to be achieved between a welfare approach and a more structural critique of existing society.

The more detailed attention given by pressure groups to specific issues replaced slogans with debate. While this could be seen as a progressive development in educational terms, it did little to resolve the old tactical tangle of how to involve the mass of the working class in a general demand for change. The ideal was invariably seen as a linking of pressure groups demands with community mobilization. Indeed the success of community groups often tended to be estimated in terms of their ability to deliver mass action. In reality it was more likely that communication was maintained through a small group of community activists who could identify issues of concern for 'their' communities. Occasionally issues 'took-off' due to popular indignation - e.g. District Heating Campaign - with active community support fluctuating on the basis of perceived success and/or publicity.

The late seventies saw the establishment of pressure groups around issues of intrinsic concern to the community movement; issues such as housing (Shelter Northern Ireland), of debt (Action on Debt), of poverty (Northern Ireland Poverty Lobby) etc. Many of the latter adopted a considerably more critical analysis of society than previously advocated by local community groups. Not that this should be surprising, given the often limited aims and perspective of the latter. Demands for radical change in such areas as the redistribution of wealth, were to provide the basis of a possible alliance with the Trade Union Movement. Extensive public spending cut-backs, spiralling unemployment and increasing poverty were to create the climate for a genuine link between local community groups, pressure groups and Trade Unions - although the ideal tended to be undermined by lack of an agreed strategy, or indeed list of priorities. Antagonism often resulted from a sense of mutual suspicion. Community activists tended to view the majority of Trade Unionists as bureaucratic and economistic. While Trade Unionists regarded the former as self-appointed and unrepresentative. The Trade Union Movement was also conscious of its vulnerable position given sectarian tensions, thus resulting in a reluctance to become involved in issues outside its immediate area of concern. The chief arena in which these mutually exclusive and defensive attitudes tended to be broken down somewhat occurred in Trades Councils throughout the Province - particularly in the relatively new or reactivated Trades Councils outside the Belfast area.

Further obstacles however were also to be encountered in the attempt to fashion an effective, class-conscious alignment. There were those groups who viewed a campaigning role as being secondary to a welfare approach, consequently they could be tethered by government funding. There were also those who feared that 'class-consciousness' might divide 'the community'. This may well be yet another reflection of the fact that the politics of Northern Ireland had done little to encourage the growth of a conscious, mass working-class movement. The influence of the large number of active Churches in the Province sanctified local preventative measures and attitudes adopted to discourage such a development.

Community Action and the Troubles

Despite the fact that the vast majority of pressure groups and of community activists spend the majority of their time and energy on issues of concern shared by working-class communities throughout Western Europe the unique problems of the Province cannot be ignored. These include the large number of men and women in prison; fears of sectarian attack or, of becoming 'an innocent victim'; harrassment by 'security' forces - official and paramilitary; the searches of houses and 'lifting' for interrogation. These are some of the many aspects of daily life experienced in working class areas of Northern Ireland. They are tolerated for the most part - regarded by many as a necessary evil; by others as an indication of continuing British Imperialism and by the majority with a sense of resigned helplessness. This was reflected in remarks from Derry and Belfast:-

> Well, I've never had any experience with the police or the army, but can see the harrassment that they give men, especially young men. But then there's the question of soldiers jeering at women - pointing guns at you, and it's frightening, you know when you see someone pointing a gun at you. And just their presence in general because you feel inhibited and frightened.

> The army kicked the door in at six o'clock in the morning and took the door right off the hinges and lifted the lad of nineteen .... I thought I was going to take a heart attack, the door just came in as I was going up the hall. They just banged it once and kicked it in ....

> .... it's about a year ago now when they had charged me and a few friends when I worked in an Advice Centre. I was in Castlereagh for a week and after being released from Castle-

reagh I had agoraphobia .... I don't go out to seek trouble with the Brits, but you get it whether you seek it or not .... For example, if you're going along and a British soldier jumps out of the shadows and demands that you open your coat and he threatens to hit you with his rifle. It has made women aware in this instance that you're going to have to defend yourself against this soldier, and make no mistake about it, it's not the first wallop I've had with a rifle.

Specific incidents involving the residents in a local area, or more general problems resulting from the continued existence of armed conflict cannot, with impunity, be overlooked by community activists in such communities.   Hence organisations such as the Bogside Community Association have been known to issue press statements reflecting local feelings about harrassment, etc.   In such circumstances the priority given to problems of more general social concern - such as rent rises - may well be considered secondary to more directly political campaigns.

Given that community action in Northern Ireland tended to be inextricably inter-connected with the political situation, developments during the Troubles resulted in two schools of thought:-

(a)   Those who saw explicit political and paramilitary involvement in community action as making the latter relevant; and

(b)   Those who sought to exclude party political elements from local community work.

Political groups and parties in turn often viewed community activity - and particularly the running of Advice Centres - as a means of gaining credibility and attracting recruits. This became, in fact, an extension of the brokerage system that has often characterised Irish politics.   Conflicting groupings, however, could result in a certain balance being achieved in communities. This problem was not as often experienced in pressure groups - as the latter were further removed from the local scene and were less likely to be an effective source of popular support.   The obvious impossibility - and perhaps even undesirability - of detaching local political forces from community action can result in the fact that the major social issue of sectarianism is politely avoided in 'mixed' community company. Nevertheless, the views expressed by individual working class men and women in 'ghetto' areas of Belfast and Derry re-emphasize the sharp reality of the sectarian divisions:-

Well, the Protestant people have a fear of the Bogside and Creggan, the Catholic Bogside and the Catholic Creggan , because we are outnumbered here in Derry, we have a fear of them dominerring us or putting us into a United Ireland.   We have to go for a Protestant Councillor, a Protestant M.P. - we can't vote for nothing else, only a Protestant because we're ignorant and the politicians are keeping us ignorant and that's the way that they have been doing this sixty years nearly, and this is why we are still at this old thing today, because we have nothing else to vote for.

Well, I feel at the present time, although I know there is a great barrier still between Protestants and Catholics, that the Protestant people are really afraid of us. They have a rather frightening notion that we are going to take over what they would term as their country . . . . I realise also that it has always been, and nobody can deny it in my opinion, that Protestants will always have their cake, while we will be lucky if we have bread and butter. That's the way the system is geared . . . .

There are those who acknowledge however that:-

. . . . having lived in a district which was predominantly Protestant in fact we were the only Catholic family in the area, we found that the people were no different than ourselves in this respect, that they enjoyed the same recreation, had the same problems, and they had the same want or lack of cash and lots of difficulties that we had . . . .

It is this premise that has inspired much of community action and attention to social issues in Northern Ireland. Activists in this area of work are also often conscious of the fact that:-

. . . . this can be taken advantage of in so far that the two communities can be worked against each other to the disadvantage of each other's interest, whereas if we had a common ground to approach each other on, namely politically, if we both understood and had open and frank discussion with each other, we would not be at the same disadvantage when dealing with authorities . . . .

The inevitable attention given to 'The Troubles' themselves tends to overshadow this 'common ground'. Community initiatives have from time to time sought to reverse this trend - although the results have not always been reassuring. As early as 1974, however, the organiser of the Bogside Community Association stressed:-

No matter what happens to the National question in the final analysis the Community struggle goes on, the struggle against the hopelessness and the helplessness of ordinary people to manage to cope in a very complex society . . . . We cannot separate politics from the community question, no matter what we try to do about it, no matter how idealistic we may be.[7]

This statement was welcomed in that it acknowledged the importance of political issues beyond those traditionally recognised in Northern Ireland. It marked an acceptance that the old mould of politics had been broken open by questions raised in the community struggle. These were the issues that were to be examined in greater detail during the course of the last decade. They were to probe far beyond the 1969 Skeffington Report's innocuous concept of 'community forums' and local participation. While there were those elements in the community movement that were content to organise local bingo and to arrange Christmas parties for the pensioners, there were others who confronted the relationship between 'politics' and the 'community question'. The result was to open local activists to the much broader debate that was described above. In short, the battle to survive in a 'society under siege' has resulted in the development of a certain strength and resourcefulness in working-class communities in Northern Ireland.

It has also provided something of a 'bridge' between the two communities suggesting that community action offers a means whereby the working class, Catholic and Protestant, can find a sense of unity and common purpose amidst deep religious and political divisions.

Thus, despite doubts amongst sociologists about the relevance of 'community' as a concept, it is one which is taken seriously by those involved in community action in Northern Ireland, and, as the American sociologist W.I. Thomas points out: 'If people define a situation as real, it is real in its consequences'. Community is regarded as real in Northern Ireland, real as a divisive force but, paradoxically, real as a force potentially capable of uniting both communities.

NOTES

1. *Belfast Areas of Special Need Report – Sub Group Report on Ballymurphy* (H.M.S.O., 1979).

2. B. Rolston, 'The Case of the Northern Ireland Community Relations Commission' (unpublished Ph.D. Thesis, Queens University, Belfast, 1978).

3. M. Hayes, *Community Relations and the role of the Community Relations Commission in Northern Ireland* (Runnymede Trust, 1972), p. 9.

4. Quoted at a conference on Politics and Community Action, Magee University College, June, 1974.

5. Ibid.

6. Report of Community Organisations Northern Ireland (Belfast, 1975).

7. Quoted at conference on Politics and Community Action, op. cit.

Chapter 5

COMMUNITY EDUCATION AND COMMUNITY ACTION
IN NORTHERN IRELAND - A CASE STUDY

Given the situation discussed in the previous chapter one would expect
that in Northern Ireland, of all places, adult education would be
concerned to explore its contribution to this process of community
development and action. However, with a few exceptions, the formal
adult education agencies in the Province operate in a very traditional
manner and, as elsewhere, cater largely for the middle class section of
the population. Notwithstanding the enormous social, economic and
political problems in Northern Ireland the organisation of adult
education reflects the general trend in modern society which results in
a concentration of resources (information, knowledge, expertise)
within institutional frameworks which are effectively divorced from
the problems faced by the great mass of the population. The emphasis
is very much on carrying on as if things were normal providing the
usual range of liberal, vocational and recreational classes.

However, the situation here is *not* normal, although this would be
hard to believe from the programme of most adult and further
education agencies! A comment from a radical educator in the
Province sums up the situation: 'Looking at the adult education
programme provided by Lausanne's University Populaire or Queen's
University, Belfast, one would not easily deduce from them that
Switzerland had a crisis of conscience about prosperity or that Belfast
had a crisis of stability'.[1] As that comment indicates, Northern
Ireland is only an extreme example of a general case. Keith Jackson
makes the same point about his first impressions of adult education in
Liverpool, suggesting that much of it was meaningless 'more like
academic parlour games than a search for understanding within the
reality of life in the city'.[2]

Two major reports on adult education in Northern Ireland,
produced during the past decade of turmoil and change, pay lip service
to the need for adult education to vigorously and positively interpret
its historic concern for social justice and equality. The most recent
report, produced by the Council for Continuing Education,[3] concludes
that: 'the central question underpinning this report, which will be
implicit in the discussions that follow and the conclusions that are
reached in this: "What is the social purpose of the Education Service,
given the reality we confront and the future we expect?" '[4]

The answer provided by the report suggests that the latter is seen principally in terms of Northern Ireland's position as a deprived region of the European Community whilst the former is seen in terms of its contribution to regional development. Thus the educational priorities singled out by the report include industrial training and retraining, leisure education for the unemployed, adult literacy, and remedial education for those with problems of identity and adjustment as a result of the 'troubles'! Social and political education is mentioned. But, it is admitted that: 'it is more difficult to tackle this item on the agenda because of the suspicion or hostility which many people feel towards educational institutions'.[5] However it is accepted that education has a role as a stimulant and catalyst in the 'troubles' in Northern Ireland. 'Whilst education cannot help solve the conflict it has a crucial role to play in helping people to understand its nature and origins and to consider the possibilities before them. On the social and economic side, the challenge is no less radical'.[6] Community education is mentioned in the report but there is no indication that the authors recognise its contribution to the sort of social and political issues outlined above. Rather it is seen very much in social-pathology terms i.e. its remedial role in deprived urban communities.

A similar view of community education is contained in a previous report from the same source 'Continuing Education for Socially Disadvantaged Areas'. 'We must begin with the recognition that continuing education with which we are concerned is more often remedial than advanced or 'recreational''.[7] However the report does recognise that such education might lead people to ask challenging questions about society and this might place tutors in an ambiguous position, especially if they became involved in organising petitions or other forms of protest. They concluded that there was no escape from this dilemma, that it was a healthy development in a democratic society. In reference to the general Northern Ireland situation the report attempts to face up to realities and states that: 'it would surely be an act of treason on the part of those who subscribe to educational values not to maintain that education has some contribution to make to the preservation, restoration, or creation of a civilized society, or to withdraw in despair from a state of affairs which is to put it mildly, so challenging'.[8]

That challenge has, in fact, been taken up by a variety of groups and individuals in Northern Ireland, many outside the formal adult education system. They operate alongside, and sometimes spring from, initiatives in community action in the province outlined in the previous chapter.

Thus Community Education Workshops, or Projects, have evolved out of local community centres or resource centres. There are a number of these scattered throughout the Province e.g. The Community Education Workshop in the staunchly Protestant working class Shankill Road area of Belfast, which arose out of the work of the local Community Council; The Community Education Programme in the predominantly Catholic Shantallow area of Derry, which arose out of the work of the local Resource Centre.

Other initiatives, like the Springhill Community House Project in the Catholic Ballymurphy area of Belfast[9] and the Open College in central Belfast, owe their origins to the efforts of specific active and committed individuals. The former attempts to provide a community education service from a base within a particular working class community. The latter attempts to offer a variety of informal classes, courses and activities from a central base for individuals and groups from communities throughout the city.

Some are the result of efforts by specific groups, e.g. the Craigavon Social Studies Group which has provided training and research for community groups in that new city[10] and the Centre for Neighbourhood Development which provides a similar service for community workers and community groups in various parts of Belfast;[11] the North Belfast Political Economy Group, which is attempting to organise research and educational support for community groups and trade unions in that declining area of the city; the Belfast Women's Law and Research Group which provides a similar service for women throughout the urban area. Other groups, like the Community Education Forum (now the Form for Community Work Education)[12] and the Art and Research Exchange, seek to provide a Province wide service for local communities and community activists. Finally, some initiatives have grown out of the work of individuals working in adult education institutions in the Province e.g. the Community Education Project at Queen's University[13], whilst a few have arisen out of a specific public commitment by the institution itself.

Like similar developments in Europe and North America these initiatives reflect a wide range of activities and corresponding educational, social, and political philosophies, sometimes explicitly stated, often not. However, they represent an alternative, popular adult education network providing traditional adult education in familiar local surroundings; educational support for community activists; research and information for the latter (numerous surveys and research reports have in fact been produced by community groups in Northern Ireland often in co-operation with committed academics[14]); community arts and writers' workshops with a strong educational component; social and political education for social, trade union and community activists.

Yet, despite this development in community education the Council for Continuing Education suggests that the two most significant educational innovations in Northern Ireland are the Open University and the Adult Literacy Project![15]

In fact the various 'community' education initiatives in Northern Ireland over the last decade reflect, fairly accurately, the four models outlined in Chapter 3. This is hardly surprising, given that Northern Ireland is not immune from general developments in educational theory and practice and the social and economic changes affecting the rest of western society.

AN INSTITUTIONAL INITIATIVE

One of the few *institutional* initiatives in community education in Northern Ireland was the decision by the New University of Ulster to establish, in 1972, an Institute of Continuing Education at Magee University College, Londonderry. It was a practical illustration, by the New University, of its concern to establish a close relationship with the Northern Ireland community. The University had decided to commit itself 'to an unusually ambitious and large scale development of community oriented education'.[16] In fact the new Institute was originally to be known as the Institute for Community Studies.

It was the largest investment by any university in adult education in Western Europe, influenced by some of the developments in community education and action in Great Britain discussed in Chapter 3, and prepared to assist in seeking solutions to the social, economic and political problems in the Province by putting its 'educational resources at the disposal of the community'.[17] Thus despite the belief voiced in the report referred to above, that it is difficult to tackle the problem of social and political education in Northern Ireland because of people's suspicion or hostility towards educational institutions, the University was comitted in principle at least, to exploring that area of adult education provision.

University adult education departments in Great Britain have, historically, sought to establish such a close relationship with their local community as a practical illustration of their sense of social responsibility. For most universities however that community has been predominantly middle class and the relationship one dominated by a narrow definition of educational 'resources' and what is, and is not, the proper domain of university adult education. However, since this was a new institute with new staff, it was possible to take these public statements of intent seriously, and to develop a community education programme in the knowledge that it was a priority for the Institute. Of course it soon became obvious that the staff had different views about what community education meant, what communities should have access to resources, what problems and issues should be tackled! This was understandable and inevitable given the fact that the commitment to community education was loose and undefined and the staff brought with them their own views and opinions about adult education. It's doubtful if, at that time, the full implications of 'community oriented education' were either understood or generally accepted. However, although there were inevitable internal conflicts in the early years it was still possible to develop such a programme specifically for working class communities.

The work at the Institute over the decade became in fact a journey, a learning process, in which views about community education and community action altered and changed in the light of theory and practice. Thus it moved through the various community education models outlined in Chapter 3. In the early years the approach was a combination of the Community Organisation and Community Development/Education models. The emphasis then changed to a Community Action/Education model and finally to a combination of the latter and the Social Action/Education model. Obviously in practice this progression was neither so systematic nor straightforward. Elements of one model were often retained and incorporated with elements from others.

COMMUNITY ORGANISATION

During this early period the concept of community oriented education, with the Institute putting its resources at the disposal of the community, rested on certain broad assumptions:-

1. That, in order to define the nature of the University's response to working class communities it was essential to establish a close working relationship with such communities. (This was made easier by the fact that the Institute was situated in close proximity to many working class communities in a relatively small city of 70,000 population).

2. That the establishment of this relationship would bring to light opportunities for assistance and resources which would not necessarily fall into conventional university adult education provision.

3. That opportunities for the creation of a comprehensive co-ordinated, community education service for the adult population in working class communities in the city would be greatly assisted by working closely with the organisations created by local activists and with other educational bodies.

4. That such 'activists' would benefit from the resources and services available in a university and that a two-way flow - the university going into working class communities and the latter going into, and making use of, the university - would greatly benefit both.

Initially members of staff made contact with a range of community groups and organisations in the city - e.g. tenants' associations, community councils, youth and community groups, pre-school groups, community resource centres, welfare rights groups, co-operative organisations - and became actively involved in their everyday work. When opportunities arose the resources and facilities in the Institute were made available to these groups, e.g. contacts with experts in particular fields in the University; information on research and material available on specific social issues and problems; access to the media resources in the Institute, i.e. radio and T.V. studios and printing facilities etc., use of rooms for meetings and discussions. Thus a serious attempt was made to open up the resources of the Institute to the community.

As a result of the contacts established during the course of this work some local community workers sought advice and assistance on educational matters. In one local community resource centre, which Institute staff had played a small part in establishing, it was decided to set up an education committee and to organise a community education service in the area. Eventually an extensive programme of fairly conventional, non-formal, classes and courses was organised by the resource centre committee in co-operation with the Institute, the W.E.A. and the local F.E. Colleges.

However, although over four hundred adults signed on for courses at a 'Meet the Providers' session in a local school most of these opted for the sort of practical, instrumental education, e.g. hairdressing, keep-fit, flower arranging, 'O' levels, etc., which is fairly typical of most community education projects. The 'liberal' adult education courses offered by the Institute did not attract many adults! However two other initiatives, one which sought to encourage working class adults from those same communities to come into the Institute for a programme of liberal studies, the other which concentrated on developing study groups in the community were much more successful.

(1) Community Studies

In 1973 a Foundation Studies Course for Mature Students was established on a one-year full-time and two-year part-time basis. The course was an introduction to liberal studies, e.g. history, social sciences, language and literature, leading to a university certificate. It was influenced by the success of the residential adult education colleges in Great Britain in attracting working class adults to full-time academic education. The Institute sought to offer a similar opportunity in Northern Ireland, but one more deeply rooted in its local community and with more provision for part-time and women students. In this way it was hoped that students would continue with their work in their own communities and thus avoid the tensions which often arise for such students when they embark on residential courses far away from family and community.

Initially the course commenced with nine full-time and thirteen part-time students. It was an immediate success even though it was liberal and academic. Soon the success of the first students (most of whom were working class) in completing the course and, in a number of cases, going on to university degree courses, was spread by word of mouth in clubs, pubs, community centres, throughout the close-knit Londonderry community! By 1978, 139 students had entered the course, 90 full-time, 49 part-time, 57% of these students were working class, 40% semi-skilled and unskilled workers. Forty per cent had taken no public examination. Yet the success rate for the full-time course was 80% and 45% for the part-time course where there was a bigger drop out rate. Most of these students went on to university.

In a city with a long history of unemployment and under-employment the course was very quickly seen in vocational terms - in the opportunities it offered for entrance to university education and a wider choice of careers. It was thus seen in terms of personal development and advancement, not collective advancement. However, it proved that traditional liberal studies could attract working class students especially if it led to some form of usable certification and that there was a huge pool of untapped ability amongst the latter. A research project on the course concluded that: 'The evidence for the existence of a, so far barely tapped, pool of intellectually able working class men and women is surely overwhelming'.[18]

63

In terms of community development and action in the city the course did not make a direct contribution to the educational needs of those involved. However, indirectly, it made a number. Thus students on the course were involved with a local resource centre in a survey of the area and an assessment of the centre's work in the community. The project work on the course (which produced some of the student's best efforts) enabled a number of them - many of whom had been active in their communities - to undertake detailed research into the history and development of the latter, to investigate a range of social and economic problems in the city, and to trace the development of various community initiatives.

In another part of the course students were introduced to the social sciences through an examination of traditional community life in Ireland and abroad and the forces - social, economic, political - responsible for the major changes experienced by such communities. Thus individual local research was linked to a broad educational programme in Community Studies.

In this way the course was able to develop links with various local communities. Often this had the effect of encouraging adults involved in community action to join the course. Thus the Institute was able, indirectly, to contribute to a deeper understanding of local problems and issues and the community was able to take advantage of the resources and opportunties available in the Institute.

Like the 'Second Chance to Learn Project in Liverpool' discussed in Chapter 3, this initiative confirmed that working class adults are capable of hard, sustained intellectual effort. It also faced some of the same problems since, although the course was seen by the tutors as an educational experience in itself and a possible contribution to local community effort, it was soon seen by the majority of students in very instrumental terms, i.e. an opportunity for entrance to higher education and wider career prospects. This is not to deny that many students had a burning desire for education which often meant that the 'content' of the course was less important than their dedication, commitment and determination. However, the 'carrot' of certification was, as research on the course showed, an extremely important element in the latter. Thus whereas Second Chance to Learn emphasised the 'content' of the course and its links with local issues and problems the Foundation Studies Course illustrated the importance of instrumentality. However, both initiatives confirmed that education for community activists could be 'academic', and that such activists were capable of undertaking research into local problems and issues. Commitment, content and instrumental value, plus close links between educators and activists, are obviously important factors in the success of such exercises. However, the fact that the students obtained grants to free them for study was also very important!

(2) Local Study Groups
Whereas the initiative discussed above was Institute based, broadly liberal and academic, this particular project was much more informal and centred in the local community. Again it grew out of contacts made whilst working with local people involved in a community

association in the city. In this case a group of women expressed an interest in the needs of pre-school children in the area and ways in which those needs could be met. A local informal study group was established in a community centre in the estate and a programme of talks and discussions agreed, and organised, by the group in association with a tutor from the Institute.[19]

Various speakers were invited to discuss aspects of child-care with the group. This was successful, as far as it went. However, it was noticeable that, initially, the group were not particularly critical of the experts they had invited. In informal discussions afterwards it became apparent that they were in disagreement with some points raised by the speakers, particularly those which were very much in contrast to their own experience as working class mothers living in a modern housing estate. There was a danger that their own lack of self-confidence in such formal situations might lead to a form of cultural invasion - a feeling of personal inadequacy as mothers.

However, this conflict of values led to an agreement to look more closely at working class community life in Londonderry and the role of women in the latter. This was done in an informal manner using the lives and experiences of the women concerned as material for their own education. They were thus able, confidently, to go back to their own past, to discuss the nature of community life and the role of women in it. This they compared with their present position as women, wives, mothers living in new housing estates where traditional community life had disappeared, creating numerous problems. 'When I came up to the Creggan to live some fifteen years ago I felt a terrible sense of isolation at the beginning. In one sense I was delighted because I had got a house, you know. It was a great thing. It had a bathroom and all which I never had in Walton Street. On the other hand I thought it a bit of a wilderness up here, you know. The place wasn't properly finished. I suppose that added to the sense of isolation about it and then I didn't know anybody for a start and I was a brave bit away from my mother and father and aunts and uncles or relatives of any kind or description. I had four children and they were all a bit of a strain. Apart from that, my husband most of the time worked in England and left me strictly on my own. I liked the scenery and I loved the house but I missed terribly the atmosphere of Walton Street. I missed my neighbours, I missed like somebody just stopping in the morning and having a wee chat with you in the street. I missed all that sort of thing'.

However most of the women did not wallow in nostalgia. They realised the need for some sort of action to solve their problems: 'Some of the young couples I would say are experiencing this feeling of isolation that I felt when I came up at the beginning but some of them are reacting to it in a different way from what I did. You have the problem of young people going out drinking, you have sort of neglect of young children arising from this situation. Young married couples are not nowadays inclined to talk out their troubles with neighbours perhaps as I was when I was young so that you have a gap between the older neighbours and the younger neighbour. When I was only up a few years and after my sixth child was born I had some trouble with my nerves which I put down more or less to being cut off entirely from my family and from my neighbourhood that I had grown up with for twenty years. I got over that all right and it was only when I got over that stage that I began to realise that we could try to make the street into the sort of community that I had lived in. So I started to approach my neighbours just that bit more. Like I made all the initial approaches anyhow to them and decided it was time that we sort of got together and started thinking about organising people. At that time some of the people in the street felt as I did and we did begin an organisation which more or less brought some people together'.

Comments like the latter illustrate that this educational process succeeded in pinpointing many of the problems facing the women in the study group - problems they all shared - and suggesting some solutions. However, it went further, it began to uncover some of the major issues and themes underlying those problems, introducing the group to cultural, sociological and historical perspectives, in family and community life. From this point on the group was freed from the topic of pre-school children. They had a glimpse of the theory of social organisation. The pre-arranged programme was completed and future meetings devoted to broader problems of community life.

They moved into various fields of action and study, as individuals and as a group. Thus some became active in setting up a local resident's association, others entered the Foundation Studies Course discussed above - something they had not contemplated before. The group took an active part in tackling the problems of information on birth control and pre-natal care for women in the estate, major problems in a city with a high birth rate! They invited various medical personnel to discuss these issues with them. However, this time they were much more confident and critical in their dealings with these 'experts'. In an evaluation of these meetings the group decided to explore the workings of the local health council, which consisted of representatives from the middle class section of the community, and to submit their own suggestions for improving health services for working class women in the city.

In assessing the success of the study group the women made it clear that they thoroughly enjoyed the experience and had gained a great deal from it. They also pointed out that the problems discussed and analysed in the group were common topics of conversation amongst women in the estate and that if education was seen in these terms and organised informally in homes and social centres many more adults would become involved in this type of community education.

This initiative indicated that, given active involvement, sensitivity, and an ability to hold a mirror to the problems and issues facing people in their everyday lives, an educational programme, similar to Freire's cultural circles, could be constructed. Such a programme could go beyond loose informal discussion by creating relevant educational material which assisted the learning process and helped create the confidence for action.

COMMUNITY DEVELOPMENT

The experience discussed above was one in which those involved were, initially, not particularly active in the community. Increased self-confidence and a new self-image sprang from their investigation of themselves and their environment. As a result they became much more active. However, during this same period, and alongside this particular activity, arose other opportunities to provide educational support for the growing number of people involved in community development.

Courses, classes, seminars, workshops were organised for the wide range of people and groups interested, or involved, in this process e.g. community development workers with the Northern Ireland Community Relations Commission, social workers, clergy, town planners, local community workers.

As far as the latter were concerned these included workshops and training courses on welfare rights and benefits; communications - including use of radio and T.V.; strategies and tactics in community work; background to community problems and issues.

Conferences were also organised bringing together represent-atives from community groups, government agencies, local authority departments, professional community workers, planners, etc., to discuss problems of common interest. This was very much a Community Development approach - an assumption that solutions to local problems would be found through dialogue and improved communication between community groups and those in authority. It rested on a belief in the educational efforts of such conferences on both parties.

SOCIAL AND COMMUNITY ACTION

Quickly community activists became disillusioned with this approach and the emphasis changed to one of community action. This in turn began to take on the shape of a potential social movement in the Province and the Institute team moved towards a combination of the community action/social action models in their educational approach to this development.

Like the experience of Highlander, discussed in Chapter 1, the work generally speaking, fell into two distinct phases. During the first phase, as the movement grew and gathered strength, it took the form of assisting those concerned in organising conferences and seminars on broad issues of common concern. This work was greatly assisted by the contacts made with local activists and the experience gained in helping with a range of community initiatives outlined above. In the second stage the work took the form of more specific workshops and courses.

This was a two-way process. Sometimes these initiatives arose from requests from community activists. On other occasions they were the result of suggestions by the educators. Usually the end result was a matter of dialogue and discussion between the two.

First Phase: Conferences and Seminars

This movement towards a community action approach culminated in 1974 in a conference on 'Politics and Community Action'. It was designed to bring together professional community workers, community activists, representatives from government agencies, local authority departments, further and higher education institutions, voluntary bodies, politicians from all over Northern Ireland, to discuss the role of community action in the Province. The government had decided to disband the Community Relations Commission, established in 1969 and active in promoting community development work in the Province. The Commission had provided resources and support for community development throughout Northern Ireland and community activists feared that its demise represented an attempt by government to stifle community action in the Province. This fear eventually proved unfounded. However, at the time, it helped create a sense of common grievance amongst the large group of Protestant and Catholic community activists from all over the Province who attended the conference. It thus offered them an opportunity to voice these grievances publicly and to discuss the future role of community development in Northern Ireland.

In fact they dominated the conference and impressed many with their optimism and idealism in a period when the country appeared on the brink of a civil war. Instead of concentrating on a community development strategy involving all the parties at the conference it became in fact, an occasion for cementing the links between community groups, highlighting their common problems and the need to organise some sort of network, a support system, for their work. However the informal contacts, the drinking, singing and general socialising, rather than the formal aspects of the conference, provided the major educational benefit. It enabled those concerned to get behind religious stereotypes and to glimpse the common problems and culture they all shared.

As a result of this experience two other conferences were organised by community activists, with help from staff at the Institute, specifically for community groups throughout Northern Ireland. They both attracted over 150 people. The first discussed, in detail, the range of common problems and issues facing community groups throughout Northern Ireland. The second resulted in the establishment of a Province-wide organisation - Community Organisations Northern Ireland - for community groups throughout the Province. However there was opposition to the proposal, aired at the conference, that this organisation should have a distinct radical, social and political philosophy, that it should help to create a social movement. Instead, in line with thinking on community development at the time and reflecting the diversity of views at the conference, it was decided that the organisation should be essentially non-directive, concerned solely with providing advice, assistance and resources for community groups.

Second Phase: Workshops and Courses

In the second phase the experiences gained in the activities discussed above proved very important. They provided the contacts, the information, the raw material for more explicit educational initiatives linked specifically to the needs of community activists and the general social, economic and cultural problems facing the working class in Northern Ireland. That experience had indicated that community action in Northern Ireland suffered from inherent contradictions and weaknesses, i.e., a lack of any clear and generally accepted social and political analysis of the problems it sought to resolve; a failure to provide and link together, in a coherent manner, an explanation of how things are, how they got that way, a vision of the future and a notion of how to get from one to the other. One commentator writing of similar experiences of community action in the U.S.A., suggests that:

> If citizen action is to catch on at a national level there will have to be that sense of channelled outrage and a collective vision of how to rectify the injustices that caused it. The bottom line of direct action organising must be the growing awareness of the largest possible number of participants in every single campaign. Campaigns may fail and organisations may die but the learning that people have internalised is for life. Once they own their new understanding they can recreate their struggle, reform groups, remobilise their friends, etc.[20]

The community action movement in Northern Ireland needed to provide such a new understanding if it was to succeed as a movement for social change. With the help of a large grant a Community Action Research and Education Project was established at the Institute in 1977. It attempted to assist the growth of that educational process.

THE C.A.R.E. PROJECT

The C.A.R.E. project set out to see how adult education might best contribute to the kind of growing social movement that working class community groups, women's groups and some trade union branches collectively composed. The team felt that such disparate initiatives contained the seeds of a movement that could transform this divided society in the long run. They also believed that such movements could not achieve their potential unless they developed educational activities to train their own members as, broadly defined, leaders and intellectuals of a new social order. Only then would sharply felt grievances and suppressed aspirations be organised into a coherent force.

They were well aware that working in Northern Ireland presented peculiar obstacles to such a movement and such educational activities. Many people argued, often with reason, that the project's approach underestimated the importance of the national struggle in Ireland. While some of that criticism was probably valid, the team were persuaded, each in his or her own way, that the long term interests of the working class throughout Northern Ireland demanded that atten-

69

tion be given to the problems that they shared with the inhabitants of capitalist societies elsewhere.

All the problems of class division, poverty, poor housing, insensitive urban planning, declining welfare services, inadequate schools and general social disadvantage are faced by the working class throughout Northern Ireland. At the same time colonial rule, religious segregation and the mess made by the imperial power in attempting to disengage from the situation, have all served to undermine any kind of effective working class movement. It may be that progress on that front proves impossible to consolidate until the national question is settled. However, the C.A.R.E. team were convinced that education which concentrated upon the common problems of the entire Northern Irish working class needed to be established as soon as possible if any hope of reconciliation and political progress were to be sustained in the long run.

At a practical level the team tried, in effect, to relate the problems facing community activists to the broader social, economic and political structures, within which their initiatives took place, to 'encourage that learning process which assists people in perceiving the cultural, social, economic and political realities affecting their lives and strengthens their capacity to transform them'.[21] Thus the C.A.R.E. team sought, in co-operation with other groups engaged in this process, to encourage the growing awareness of the largest possible number of participants through a radical comprehensive response to community issues and problems.

This entailed active involvement in, and commitment to, community action in the Province, not simply as 'non-directive' resource providers but critical participants with an important service, education, to contribute to the process. This contribution was one which, whilst recognising the imporant role of 'academic' education for those involved in community action, accepted that it could only be part of a broad educational response to the latter. On the basis of the experiences outlined above, it sought therefore to develop the concept of 'cultural action'; to provide training in skills relevant to community action; to develop a role for research in the latter; all in all exploring ways in which the acquisition of skills, information and knowledge could be linked to the needs of community activists in a manner which combined the practical, the intellectual and the cultural.

The case studies discussed in the following chapters illustrate the problems and difficulties the team faced in attempting this approach to the provision of education for community action in Northern Ireland. A major part of that approach was the need to encourage a process of reflection on community action in the Province.

NOTES

1.   D. Wilson 'The Role of Adult Education in a Working Class Community with special reference to the Springhill Community House Project, Belfast', (unpublished M.A. dissertation, New University of Ulster, 1978) p. 16.

2.   K. Jackson, in J.L. Thompson (Ed.), *Adult Education for a Change*, (Hutchinson, London, 1980), p. 13.

3.   *Continuing Education in Northern Ireland - a strategy for development*, A Report of the Council for Continuing Education, (H.M.S.O., Northern Ireland), 1980.

4.   Ibid., p. 35.

5.   Ibid., p. 21.

6.   Ibid., p. 21.

7.   *Report of the Panel on the Socially Disadvantaged*, Council for Continuing Education, (H.M.S.O., Northern Ireland, 1978), Para. 7, p. 2.

8.   Ibid., para. 9, p. 3.

9.   D. Wilson, op. cit.

10.   *Community School* - A Report from the Craigavon Social Studies Group (Craigavon, Northern Ireland), 1976.

11.   *The Centre for Neighbourhood Development - An Assessment* (Industrial Training Services, Belfast), 1980.

12.   *Final Report of the Community Education Forum* (Community Education Forum, Belfast), 1981.

13.   F. Gaffakin, S. Griffiths, D. Ray and D. Rowlands, *Report of a Community Education Project 1976-78* (Queens University, Belfast), 1979.

14.   See for example, A. Spencer, *Ballymurphy, a tale of two surveys* (Queens University, Belfast) 1973; E. Evason, *'Just me and the Kids' - a study of single parent families in Northern Ireland* (Equal Opportunities Commission, Belfast), 1980.

15.   *Continuing Education in Northern Ireland*, op. cit.

16.   *1973 Brochure*, New University of Ulster Institute of Continuing Education.

17.   Ibid.

18.   F. D'Arcy, S. Courtney and T. Lovett, 'The Working Class and assess to Higher Education' (unpublished paper, Institute of Continuing Education, Londonderry, 1982) p. 11.

19.   T. Lovett and L Mackay, 'Community Based Study Groups', *Adult Education*, Vol. 51, No. 1 (May, 1978).

20.   J. Perlman, 'Seven Voices from One Organisation:- What does it mean' (unpublished paper, University of Southern California, 1980) p. 18.

21.   P. Freire, *Cultural Action for Freedom* (Penguin, Harmondsworth, 1972) p. 51.

Chapter 6

REFLECTION ON ACTION

'The starting point for organising the programme of content of education or political action must be the present, existential concrete situation, reflecting the aspirations of the people. Utilising certain basic contradictions, we must pose this existential present situation to the people as a problem which challenges them and requires a response - not just at the intellectual level, but at the level of action'.[1]

In Northern Ireland that 'existential concrete situation' posed certain basic contradictions for those involved in community action in the Province, in particular the gap between their hopes and aspirations and the reality of their achievements. As Freire has emphasised, unless those involved in various forms of social and political action engage in their own praxis then their activities will remain marginal to the forces shaping and maintaining society. They will not have an opportunity to 'speak their word' which, as he stresses, implies the right 'of creating and recreating, of deciding and choosing and ultimately participating in society's historical process'.[2]

The C.A.R.E. project actively sought to encourage such a praxis, a process of reflection on the experiences of community action in the Province during the 1970's.

In attempting this reflective process the C.A.R.E. team occupied no special privileged position other than that of committed participants in community action. However they had gained certain practical insights into the problems, difficulties and contradictions facing community activists in the Province. They had also gained some insight into the perception people held of the world around them. Freire understood the necessity of such experience and insights for those involved in radical education: 'This task implies that revolutionary leaders do not go to the people in order to bring them a message of salvation but in order to come to know through dialogue both about their objective situation and their awareness of that situation - the various levels of perception of themselves and of the world in which and with which they exist. One cannot expect positive results from an educational or political action programme which fails to respect the particular view of the world held by people. Such a programme constitutes cultural invasion good intentions notwithstanding'.[3]

The team had come to know, through dialogue and action, about the objective situation facing those involved in community action in Northern Ireland and about their awareness of it. They sought to use the contradictions in that situation as a problem which would challenge those involved, requiring a response at an intellectual level and at the level of action. However the problem with any attempt to encourage reflection on community action is that it is only a small part of the objective situation of those involved. Their experiences in family life, school, church, trade unions, political parties, play an overwhelming role in shaping their view of the world. As American studies have indicated, participating in community action does not necessarily result in a reinterpretation of the world by those concerned.[4] They are often able to live with certain basic contradictions, i.e. on the one hand the knowledge gained by active community involvement, of basic social and economic injustices and, on the other hand, their own traditional conservative values. In fact, many of the community activists interviewed in American studies were opposed to overall views of the world and regarded themselves as non-ideological or even anti-ideological.

That situation has many similarities with that of those involved in community action in Northern Ireland; the same anti-ideological or non-ideological stance; the same populist approach; the same set of contradictions and inconsistencies between radical hopes and aspirations and conservative values and attitudes. In Great Britain the labour/trade union tradition, provides for many community activists, a coherent ideology, a political consciousness, i.e. 'a coherent viewpoint providing an interpretive framework for the understanding of relations between society, culture and political economy'.[5]

That tradition is not so influential in community action in Northern Ireland. Other political, religious and cultural forces - outside community action - are much more important influences in creating a world view for those involved in that process. These have their roots in nationalist and unionist history and mythology. Thus, in attempting to encourage reflection on community action in Northern Ireland, it is necessary to tackle, not only many of the social and economic *issues*, but also the political and cultural 'themes' underlying the world view of those involved in that process.

In particular it is essential to encourage more discussion and analysis of those cultural themes which form the basis of many important myths which influence and shape thinking and action in Northern Ireland. Freire recognised the tendency for such themes to be mythicised 'establishing a climate of irrationality and sectarianism' - a description which certainly fits certain aspects of the conflict in Northern Ireland! To tackle this problem he suggested that: 'In such a situation myth-creating irrationality itself becomes a fundamental theme. Its opposing theme, the critical and dynamic view of the world, strives to unveil reality, unmask its mythicisation and achieve a full realisation of the human task'.[6]

Of course any adult education project can only expect to make a small contribution to such a daunting task! Other individuals and groups in Northern Ireland, and abroad, have been involved in this important work for over a decade. Their efforts are always at the mercy of the continuing conflict and the passions and divisions it engenders in, and between, both communities. Also, compared to the total institutional resources provided for traditional further and adult education in the Province, this work is very much a minority activity - although this is not to underestimate its influence.

In such situations faith and hope are essential requirements. Faith in the people, in their ability to 'create and recreate and to become more fully human'. Such a faith is strained to the limits in the situation prevailing in Northern Ireland. However, there are numerous instances of people reaching across the divide to assist each other and to frankly discuss their differences. Community action, despite all its weaknesses, has created many such opportunities, thus strengthening that faith in the people here. Hope is also essential. Hope in the future, in the possibility of creating a new, just society, out of injustices and divisions of the present order. However, as indicated above, that new order cannot be achieved without critical thinking, without a praxis of action and reflection.

Three factors in community action, it is claimed, can encourage that critical thinking and thus lead those involved to a re-interpretation of the world around them: i.e. action, interpretation and internalisation.[7] The action must be such that it challenges the normal course of things. If this does not occur and activists are constantly engaged in mundane community affairs then there is no material experience on which to base re-interpretation. The latter implies that the organisation concerned gives attention to learning from failures and victories, to open discussion and analysis before and after such actions. Internalisation is the process by which the lessons learnt from action and interpretation are incorporated into personal attitudes and behaviour outside community action. This is more likely to occur in groups where the leadership has some degree of ideological clarity, where there is a process of internal discussion and a high degree of solidarity and friendship with friends, neighbours and relatives also in the organisation.

In Northern Ireland, during the early 70's many people - on both sides of the religious divide - were involved in community action which challenged the normal course of things, especially during those periods, discussed in previous chapters, when no-go areas were established and community groups effectively 'controlled' their districts. Some degree of reinterpretation did take place as a result of reflection on this experience, even amongst those involved in para-military activity! Thus a spokesman for a Protestant para-military group commented that: 'We are aware that socially and economically we have more in common with our opposite number on the Republican side than we have with the loyalist big wigs. But how are we going to put this over? What formula are we going to find to get the ordinary people of Ulster to vote on real issues which concern them and not on the entrenched sectarian issues into which they have been brain-washed?'[8]

Unfortunately this realisation of the common plight of Catholics and Protestants, as a result of involvement in community action, has not been accompanied by any radical reinterpretation of the situation here - providing an alternative political consciousness - a coherent ideology. The cultural influences outside the experiences of community action, briefly outlined above, and the internal divisions and conflicts within community organisations, limit the degree of ideological clarity. However, Northern Ireland has had its fair share of outsiders who have attempted to provide an alternative ideology for those community activists who had abandoned their previous view of the situation here and sought a more radical interpretation. Often this has taken the form of a group therapy approach focussing on interpersonal relationships and change through a process of psychological and emotional upheaval, attempting to 'psychologise' Ulster into peace. The results are often disastrous.[9]

The C.A.R.E. project rejected this approach and concentrated, not on the people themselves, but on the interpretation of action and on the analysis of the major themes underlying their common problems, the divisions and the contradictions facing working class people in the Province. This process of 'reflection' was conducted at two levels. The first concentrated on community action and related issues. It involved the relatively small group of people actively involved in that process. The second concentrated on cultural values and attitudes, using local radio as a resource in an attempt to reach a larger section of the working class in the Province.

To encourage reflection on community action the project organised a series of workshops and conferences on a variety of problems and issues relevant to community action in Northern Ireland. Generally speaking these fell into two categories. The first concentrated on broad issues and themes, bringing together community activists from all over the Province with those involved in other forms of social and political action e.g. trade unionists, political activists, and those concerned with various issues in the Province, e.g. human rights, poverty, one-parent families, housing, womens aid, etc. The second concentrated more specifically on community organisations, and the internal problems and issues confronting those active in the latter.

This approach to the educational needs of social and community activists was central to the work of the Highlander Centre, mentioned briefly in Chapter 1. Highlander concentrated on short-term residential workshops as a means of helping people to solve their problems. It encouraged reflection on action whilst at the same time being actively involved itself in supporting that action. The emphasis in such workshops was on group problem-sharing which fostered co-operation and mutuality and encouraged the growth of social movements. The workshops sought to strike broad themes which pointed to the external forces responsible for the problems facing those involved and the inevitability of political and economic conflict in the search for solutions to those problems.

Highlander was not neutral. It had a radical ideological position and actively sought to provide, not only an explanation of how things were and how they got that way, but a 'vision' of what it might become and how this might be achieved. Its methods were strongly democratic, emphasising joint decision-making in education. This led to an explicit anti-academic bias in its approach. 'Every conventional learning device of academic accords is discarded. Highlander workshops are vigorously non-academic. This is imperative'.[10]

'ISSUE' WORKSHOPS

C.A.R.E. workshops whilst sharing many of the features of, and principles underlying, Highlander's work were not so 'vigorously anti-academic'. The experience of the previous five years at the Institute had indicated that there was a role for an 'academic' approach in community education. In fact the first workshop organised by the project sought purposefully to encourage such an approach. It brought together a range of well known community activists from various parts of the Province to reflect on their experiences of community action during the 70's. It was a deliberate attempt to explore openly the link between ideas and action. Prior to this particular initiative many of those involved, like their American counterparts, denied that they had any 'philosophy', any 'ideology'. They expressed suspicion of those who did, regarding them as 'academics', 'socialists', 'marxists', who had closed minds, attempting to 'impose' their views of the world on others.

In fact as Edward Thompson points out there is some foundation for such suspicions. He suggests that: 'what Marxism might do, for a change, is sit on its own head a little in the interests of socialism's heart. It might close down one counter of its universal pharmacy, and cease dispensing potions of analysis to cure the maladies of desire. This might do good politically as well since it would allow a little space, not only for literary utopians, but also for the unprescribed initiatives of everyday men and women, who, in some part of themselves, are also alienated and utopian by turns'.[11]

Gramsci, of course, recognised the problems and difficulties involved for those who seek to initiate a discussion of ideologies, to explore the link between ideas, culture and action. 'A philosophy of praxis cannot but present itself at the outset in a polemical and critical guise, as superseding the existing mode of thinking and existing concrete thought (the existing cultural world). First of all, therefore, it must be a criticism of 'common sense' basing itself entirely, however, on common sense in order to demonstrate that 'everyone' is a philosopher and that it is not a question of introducing from scratch a scientific form of thought into everyone's individual life, but of renovating and making critical an already existing activity'.[12]

As indicated above the C.A.R.E. project had earned some right to initiate this 'reflective' process because of its active involvement in community action, its insight into some of the problems and contradictions in the latter, and its knowledge of the common sense view of those involved. It sought in this first reflective workshop to indicate that, contrary to their expressed views and opinions, those concerned were 'philosophers' in Gramsci's sense of the term, that their actions were informed by some view of the world, by their social construction of reality.

In fact, despite their suspicion of 'theorists', 'academics', 'marxists', this particular workshop was welcomed by many leading activists in the Province. The failures of community action in the 70's had created a sense of disillusionment. There was general feeling that it had not lived up to expectations, that it had lost its sense of direction and that a period of reassessment was necessary.

In order to assist this reassessment, to explore the links between ideas and action, a number of participants were asked to write papers briefly outlining their experiences of community action, their analysis of its weaknesses and strengths, their 'way forward'. These papers were then distributed to the other participants in the workshop. It was felt that committing ideas and experiences to paper would itself be a learning process, a contribution to a personal praxis, offering those concerned an opportunity to 'renovate and made critical an already existing activity'. They would thus be able to 'capture' their ideas and experiences, to face up to them and develop them in a manner not always possible in dialogue and discussion. As part of this reflective process the project included its own paper based on experiences at the Institute.[13]

The workshop did not result in any general agreement about 'the way forward'. None was expected. However it did succeed in creating an atmosphere of open and honest reflection and reassessment, generally unhampered by personality conflicts. Some Protestant participants added a historic note to the workshop pointing out that community action was not new in Northern Ireland, that the Labour Movement and the trade unions had united working people - Protestants and Catholics - before, only to be driven apart by green and orange ideologies. They saw community action in terms of its contribution to eventual working class unity: 'We see our role to unitedly stand against sectional and divisive interests and by our actions prove that all communities can contribute to peace and stability'. Others stressed the extent to which aspects of community action in Northern Ireland had been 'revolutionary' giving local communities control over resources, e.g. patrolling their own districts, arranging for its defence, opening schools, looking after refugees, elderly, and children, setting up their own local institutions. However, traditional authority had stepped in and taken it over: 'There were few who knew what was happening, but now it seems that the authorities of both church and state realised better than the people that a real revolution had taken place - 'the lost revolution' - and that control had to be taken back at once'.

This sense of a lost 'opportunity' was the main theme in many of the papers and in the discussions which took place during the workshop. However there was disagreement on the analysis of the situation facing activists; on the reasons for this lost opportunity; on the prescriptions offered for the way forward. Often the belief in the need for radical solutions was not matched by any radical in-depth analysis linking together coherently an explanation of how things were, how they got that way and how they could be improved except in terms of 'them and us', 'bureaucracy', 'particpation', 'co-ordination'. Perlman in her study of American community action groups found a similar situation. She used Hobsbawm's distinction between 'pre-political' thought as distinct from 'political consciousness' to characterise the situation.

The latter, according to Hobsbawm, is a 'coherent viewpoint providing an interpretive framework for the understanding of relations between society, culture and political economy'.[14] In contrast pre-political thought is seen as less coherent, with little conception of long range goals or programmes. It responds in a fragmented fashion to immediate grievances and frequently sees little relationship between the concrete problem at hand and the larger social system.

Most of the participants at the workshop fitted somewhere between these two extremes, whilst some were at the poles! They had radically different views about community action. Generally speaking there were three different approaches, i.e. a 'welfare service' approach which accepted the ways things are but sought to improve the quality of community life by putting pressure on government and local authorities to 'humanise' their services to the community; a 'human growth' approach which recognised the need for fundamental changes in society but thought this would occur through personal growth and improved inter-personal relations; a socialist/political approach which also recognised the need for dramatic changes in society but located the key to such changes in the institutions which control political and economic power.

These three broad approaches reflected very different views of history, human beings and social change. Those in the welfare service approach felt that the giant decisions of economic planning and the intimate ones of personal self-fulfilment were up to others. Both national and personal spheres were considered beyond the scope of community groups. They wanted to concentrate instead on providing a humane welfare society, compensating for some of the inadequacies of the welfare state by seeking participation in the daily implementation of welfare policies at local level. This entailed some dealings with government but they did not expect to influence the major policy framework of the state.

Those in the human growth approach similarly also expected to develop in relative isolation from the large scale decisions about unemployment, income distribution, investment, etc. They did so on the grounds that their initial task was to help people to change themselves and their personal relationships. They felt that when this was achieved society would also change. Theirs was not therefore a Freire type approach to social change since it located the source of the problems inside people rather than in the larger society.

The final group, those in the socialist political approach, whilst supporting local community action, rejected the basic social and political assumptions underlying the views of the other two. For these activists the working class must necessarily be organised to confront and radically transform centralised power. The main division at the workshop was between this socialist approach and the other two. The workshop did not have the time to analyse and discuss these various approaches in any detail. That would have taken more than one weekend! However there was a general feeling that, despite their

78

differences, these three approaches could, and should, be combined to offer a new radical ideology to guide and direct community action.

Despite this loose consensus it was also obvious that there was still a gulf between Catholic and Protestant community activists; that deep-seated fears, suspicions, stereotypes still existed; that the emphasis on 'common' problems often obscured the need to explore more openly those fears and suspicions. For instance many Protestant activists were opposed to community action becoming a social movement because it would arouse suspicions amongst their co-religionists and comparisons with the Civil Rights 'movement', which was widely regarded by the latter as a Republican front. On the other hand Catholics were often unaware of the difficult position this created for Protestants in their own communities.

Catholics, on the whole, had a much firmer grasp of social and political realities, assisted no doubt by the variety of radical social and political groups in Catholic communities which had sprung up as a result of their position as a disadvantaged minority. Protestants, in the main, did not have the same sense of radical political roots, the same confident grasp of social reality. This is not to deny that such roots existed, as the comments by two Protestant activists at the workshop on the Labour and trade union movement indicated. However this was a hidden history for many Protestant activists obscured by their subordinate position in the Orange system. They were often unduly influenced, in their search for a social construction of reality to explain the issues and contradictions they experienced in community action, by the explanations offered by the 'outsiders' referred to above, rather than a re-examination of their working class radical roots.

Thus the workshop, although not successful in obtaining any detailed consensus regarding the way forward, did indicate a number of areas and themes which obviously required further reflection and action. These included:-

(a) A more open discussion of religious stereotypes and their origins.
(b) An examination of political views and opinions, particularly regarding the future of Northern Ireland.
(c) A detailed analysis of the background to community problems and the different strategies of community action expressed at the workshop.
(d) An attempt to forge links between 'community' action and other forms of social, political and trade union action.

Some of these issues were taken up by the project and explored in various aspects of its work. Thus, for example, a workshop was organised on political options in Northern Ireland. This was a deliberate attempt to engage people in open discussion about their political differences and the various options offered as solutions to those differences, e.g. integration with Great Britain, federation with the rest of Ireland, independence for Ulster.

One initial problem regarding this particular workshop was that some sources were not particularly happy about holding it in the

Institute. Apparently it was regarded as a 'hot potato', a sensitive issue, which might provide a vehicle for open sectarianism. Visions of mad Ulstermen and women physically battling with each other on university property may have been uppermost in people's minds!

This stereotype did in fact raise itself at the workshop, when it was eventually organised (in co-operation with the Community Education Project at Queen's University) at Corrymeela, the Christian reconciliation centre in Northern Ireland. However it did not emerge in the actions of the participants but in the comment of a visitor to the conference - an English clergyman who happened to be staying for a short period at Corrymeela.

The workshop brought together a range of community activists and people involved in politics in the Province. They listened to a range of papers on the various options and discussed these in small groups. Again there was no consensus, no agreement, but issues were discussed openly and honestly. Divisions and differences were not avoided. It was this very situation which surprised the clergyman. He commented that it was completely contrary to the stereotype portrayed in England, where it was assumed Protestants and Catholics were incapable of rational dialogue and discussion about their differences! However, although the workshop gave the lie to that particular stereotype it did not attempt to reach deep into the nature and origins of the stereotypes of themselves and the 'other sort' held by the participants. Nevertheless it indicated that such an exploration was both necessary and possible.

Other workshops sought to establish links with those involved in various forms of social, political and trade union action in the Province. They included one on Human Rights in Northern Ireland. This was an attempt to bring together the range of groups and individuals involved in seeking human rights, in a variety of areas, e.g. social, economic, political, sexual, etc. It offered community activists an opportunity to explore the relationship between their work and that of those involved in seeking justice and equality for trade unionists, women, the poor, the unemployed, the low paid, homosexuals, political prisoners. Again it was possible to engage in a rational discussion about these issues although it was something of a surprise for some to note that those with radical views on the problem of 'political' prisoners had very conservative views about the whole issue of sexual freedom!

The workshop was a limited success, indicating some of the problems and contradictions involved in the search for human rights in Northern Ireland. However it succeeded in establishing contacts between various groups and individuals. As a result a number of other conferences and workshops were organised which tackled, in more detail, some of the issues at the human workshop, e.g. poverty, housing, women's aid, one-parent families, economic cuts. Arising out of these workshops a number of practical initiatives were undertaken to establish a women's aid centre, a pre-school centre, a local co-operative job creation scheme, a law centre.

PROBLEM WORKSHOPS

Whereas the workshops discussed above concentrated on broad issues and themes the other category of reflective workshops organised by the project dealt with the practical problems facing specific community groups and organisations. Many of these problems had to do with the relationship between the objectives of those organisations and their existing role and structure. Inevitably the deeper conflicts, divisions and contradictions about community action highlighted in the 'issue' workshops, were never far from the surface.

However, although the latter obviously influenced the internal structure of community organisations, and the strategies and methods they adopted, these were seldom openly debated. Instead they usually took the form of personality clashes, or confrontations between different groupings for influence and control. Often the man, or woman, in the middle was the full-time community worker employed by such organisations. They have to cope with the internal 'politics' of the latter. This often meant that they were placed on a tight rein by the committee and had to tread very warily. It also placed them in a difficult position regarding the policies and strategies they could pursue since these were seldom openly clarified. The exceptions were those local community workers who had played an important role in setting up a community association and/or exercised a strong influence on its strategy and policy during its formative years. The problem then was exactly the opposite - i.e. how could the ordinary members exercise some influence and control over their employee!

Thus in the latter situation there was often a great deal of action but little participation and the members of the community group learnt little about the practical meaning of community work. In the former situation it was the opposite problem, too little action, because there was too much participation, too much time taken up with argument and debate. Perlman discussing similar problems amongst community groups in the U.S.A. quotes Martin Oppenheimer: 'A paradox exists between the democratic content of a group and the progress of the group towards a measure of power in the community. Too much discussion we stop moving; too little and we are no longer what we were. To achieve a goal we need unity but to achive unity it is sometimes necessary to compromise, to gloss over important issues - which shall it be?'.[15]

In practice compromises are usually made and open political discussion and debate avoided because they threaten the very structure of community organisations. This is inevitable in Northern Ireland where - despite outward appearances - there are major conflicts and divisions within Catholic and Protestant communities.

A study of two community organisations, one in the Catholic Bogside area of Londonderry, the other in the Protestant Finaghy area of Belfast, stressed this point: 'The experience of both the Bogside and Finaghy shows that in a community that is already deeply divided politically (and where rival political (and military) organisations are seeking to win some measure of popular support, many people will be genuinely suspicious of the reasons why members of political or paramilitary groups should want to be involved in community groups. The disagreements that such groups engender can often hinder a community group from initiating community action as they try to cope with their political differences. Equally, if a community association is thought to be dominated by one group to the exclusion of others, that too can limit the ability of that association to initiate 'community action''.[16]

This situation is not confined to Northern Ireland as Perlman's study emphasises: 'Political awareness requires political discussion but political discussion can be divisive. Organisers who lived through the 1960's saw the left fragment itself into impotence over the correct line! With most of them being middle class, white, educated males already committed to progressive politics it was hard enough to find common cause. Imagine the difficulties of doing this with a community group of mixed race, class, age and political experience'.[17]

Thus the reflective workshops organised by the project had to tread very carefully! Many were requested by community organisers and organisations because of their involvement in the larger community action 'issue' workshops discussed above. However, for the reasons outlined, these workshops proved much more difficult and often much less successful. At Highlander they experienced similar problems and difficulties, particularly those to do with interest and power blocks, personality conflicts, and the tendancy of some prominant activists to dominate discussion.[18] These often got in the way of the reflective process. However, although Highlander rejected academic methods it placed great stress on the need for clear educational structures and process in order to counter these problems. Staff at Highlander had their own educational agenda which helped them to clarify the structure, process and educational goals of their work. Thus although the workshops they organised were essentially democratic, duplicating and building on the natural learning process of the people involved, the staff were in no doubt about their role, i.e., the need to keep ahead of the group, threading their way through a maze of information, facts, distortions, personal needs and assumptions. They attempted to strike broad themes, to stress the importance of external forces in the problems facing activists, to build banks and channels to keep the flow of discussion and debate moving.

The C.A.R.E. project team attempted to build similar banks and channels in the workshops they organised. However this did not prove so easy when those involved were members of local community organisations. Thus a number of workshops which were arranged to help local community organisations to look more closely at their role and function, to examine their structure and organisation, ran into problems. These had mainly to do with the reluctance of those concerned to let the project provide a structure which would have assisted the learning process. Unlike the larger issues workshops, where questions of influence and control were not in dispute, this was often central to the problems facing local community groups and they were not prepared to have their hidden agendas examined openly for fear that it would break the implicit consensus of the group. Thus on some occasions the project team were allowed only a minimum control of the educational agenda and the workshops did not succeed in highlighting the major issues and problems facing the particular community association concerned.

On other occasions when the project team were given some degree of control over the learning process it was possible to achieve much greater participation and open debate. However such successes were not achieved without a degree of conflict between the team and the organisation concerned as the former strove to assure the latter that 'control' of the educational structure and process did not imply that the team would determine the outcome of the workshop, but would seek only to assist the reflective process.

Such successes were limited however by the very nature of the contradictions discussed above i.e. open debate on the hidden political and social viewpoints of the participants would have threatened the existence of the group, but the very lack of broadly agreed social and political viewpoints meant that it was extremely difficult for the group to pursue a coherent and dynamic community action strategy. The participants in these workshops confined themselves to identifying the particular local issues and problems they should tackle and in what order of priority. However they were reluctant to discuss questions of broad strategy and the relationships between the latter and their structure, organisation and role.

CONCLUSION

Although this aspect of the project's work was thus a limited success in terms of any radical reappraisal of community action in Northern Ireland, at a local and Province wide level, it did encourage a certain amount of reflection and discussion amongst those involved in the latter. It highlighted some of the contradictions and the divisions in community action, although it did not resolve them! It produced some new insights and encouraged some practical initiatives.

However the C.A.R.E. project learnt a great deal from this reflective process. It learnt that social and political education requires time, effort, patience and sensitivity, that it is no overnight process but one demanding long term commitment and resources. At the more practical level it learnt not to confuse democratic participation in community education with lack of structure, and concern for educational goals, processes and content. Concern with the latter became a major part of the project's other efforts to relate adult education to community action. The experience also highlighted the need to encourage a process of reflection on cultural values and attitudes, and to engage in a form of 'cultural action'.

NOTES

1. P. Freire, *Pedagogy of the Oppressed* (Penguin, Harmondsworth, 1972), p. 68.
2. Ibid., p. 30.
3. Ibid., p. 68.

4.   J. Perlman, 'Seven voices from one organisation: What does it mean?' (unpublished paper, University of Southern California, 1980).

5.   Ibid., p. 20.

6.   Freire, op. cit., p. 74.

7.   Perlman, op. cit.

8.   Quoted in *Sunday News*, Belfast, 2/1/1977.

9.   M. Chinoy, "How not to solve a crisis", *New Society*, 4/9/1975.

10.   M. Clark, "Meeting the Needs of the Adult Learner: Non-formal Education for Social Action", in *Convergence*, Vol. XI, 1978, p. 6.

11.   E.P. Thompson, *William Morris; Romantic to Revolutionary* (revised ed.) (Merlin Press, London, 1977) p. 807.

12.   Q. Hoare and G.N. Smith (Eds.), *Selections from the Prison Notebooks of Antonio Gramsci* (Laurence and Wishart, London, 1973), p. 331.

13.   T. Lovett and R. Percival, "Politics, Conflict and Community Action in Northern Ireland" in P. Curno (Ed.), *Political Issues and Community Work* (Routledge and Kegan Paul, London, 1978).

14.   Perlman, op. cit.

15.   Ibid., p. 17.

16.   Lovett and Percival, p. 185.

17.   Perlman, p. 17.

18.   Clark, op. cit.

Chapter 7

'CULTURAL' ACTION AND THE MEDIA

Cultural Action

In the general debate about community education and community action many experienced activists and educators have expressed dissatisfaction with the failure of both activities to come to grips with the cultural revolution, with the tremendous changes in moral attitudes and values and in social behaviour to be found in most working class communities. This is a field which has been left in most instances to the women's movement or to social workers and group therapists.

One commentator, writing about British experience, points out that although community workers operate in this domestic sphere they are not closely involved in assisting those concerned to explore the issues raised by this cultural revolution. They should accept that community action is about such things and take them on in a more systematic way possibly in a network of informal groups using a Freire type educational method. In this way the 'politics of personal life' as he calls it, can be linked to larger political concerns.[1] Miliband makes the same point in his emphasis on the new demand for more democratic relations in daily life. He feels that this cultural revolution will form an intrinsic part of any new radical social order.[2]

In the U.S.A. there is the same concern to include this cultural revolution in the themes and issues discussed, and tackled, by community groups and workers. There is increasing emphasis on value-based, rather than issue-based, organisations; on 'bottom up dialogue' and consciousness raising using Freire type methods; reinforcing ties of culture, trust and community within groups and institutions, focussing on a sense of 'we' rather than 'them'. 'People feel concerned about the loss of traditional guidelines, culture and value in their lives and are as able to talk about this as they are to complain about the garbage in the street or the needed stop sign on the corner'.[3] Groups involved in this process are concerned to ask the right questions; to build up a process of popular education; to combine an exploration of the 'why', the 'what' and the 'how' before embarking on any form of community action.

In an attempt to provide such a popular education there has emerged over the last decade a set of disparate activities under the general heading of 'community arts' e.g. community arts workshops, writers workshops, community video, radio and T.V., community press, off-set printing, duplicating, etc. Linking them all is a belief that cultural activity and social action are not distinct and separate but aspects of the same process, the former contributing to the latter.

The emphasis in such activities is two-fold. One, to demystify the arts and the nuts and bolts of the communications media so that they can be used by the working class to highlight the issues and problems they face, to become in effect, a 'resource' for social and community action. Two, to enable the working class to utilise aspects of their own culture, history and tradition, for their own education. 'Cultural policies will be trivial and marginal unless they help the working class to regain control of their own culture, including the mass media and help them to develop a critical spirit and create for themselves significant styles of life'.[4]

Thus many community arts projects have been concerned to assist working class communities to explore their own history, write their own books, record their own past, make their own T.V. and radio programmes, develop their own theatre, print their own newspapers. In this respect they can be seen as part of that older radical tradition discussed in Chapter 1, but attempting to use modern means of communication.

The main criticism of this development is similar to that directed at community education, i.e. that in concentrating on the cultural competence of the working class there is a danger that the larger cultural capital will be ignored; that they will not be introduced to the wealth of films, plays, books, paintings, which can act as triggers to the imagination and social consciousness; that it can develop a sort of inverse cultural snobbery.

What is required is a combination of the two, an attempt to develop working class competence and confidence in all the fields referred to above, plus an introduction to the wider cultural inheritance, to assist people to say their own word and to let them hear the voice of those who speak to them of their own experiences through traditional cultural forms. Freire recognised this distinction. Thus, although he stressed the value of using the culture and voices of the people for their own education, he also realised the importance of the artist in this process. 'The Brazilian novelist Gumaraes Rosa is a brilliant example of how a writer can capture authentically, not the pronunciation or the grammatical corruptions of the people, but their syntax; the very structure of their thought. Indeed (and this is not to disparage his exceptional value as a writer) Gumaraes Rosa was the investigator par excellence of the 'meaningful thematics' of the inhabitants of the Brazilian Hinterland'.[5]

John Berger makes a similar point in discussing the painter Millet, 'The pride with which a class first sees itself depicted in a permanent art is full of pleasure, even if the art is flawed and the truth harsh. The depiction gives an historic resonance to their lives. A pride which was before an obstinate refusal of shame becomes an affirmation'.[6] Many working class social activists can bear witness to the truth of that statement and the influence exerted on their intellectual development by - to name but a few - the novels of D.H. Lawrence, Upton Sinclair, Jack London. In modern terms, T.V. drama series like 'Days of Hope' and 'Roots' probably have had the same effect.

The C.A.R.E. project in entering this field of cultural activity and action decided therefore to encourage these two aspects of the work. Thus the project was responsible for setting up a community arts group involving working class artists from various parts of the city. It organised a community arts exhibition and provided printing and duplicating for a local community arts magazine. It made the T.V. and radio and video facilities in the college available to local groups. A number produced their own video films of local problems and issues. Some used the T.V. and radio studios to make their own programmes or to rehearse for a spot on local radio or T.V. However, the project also placed great stress on the use of drama and literature in the general education and training programme for community activists discussed in later chapters. For many local community workers the introduction to novels about working class life provided that 'historic resonance' referred to by John Berger.

COMMUNITY RADIO

The project was greatly assisted in all this 'cultural activity' by the wide range of resources in the Institute and by its ability, not without some struggle, to make them available to community groups and activists. However the major resource which the project sought to utilise for this work was local radio. Much experiment and debate has gone on about community radio, as well as community T.V. and video, and its role in stimulating reflection and action.[7] The more radical supporters see it as offering exciting new possibilities for community participation in, and possible control of, aspects of the media, similar to that sought in education and welfare. They regard the mass media as another aspect of increasing bureaucratisation and centralisation in society encouraging the individual's sense of isolation and cultural inferiority. Participation in the media is seen as a means whereby a different vision of society can be presented, breaking down that sense of isolation and inferiority, stimulating self-confidence, encouraging a new sense of community and a radically different set of social relationships.

There is little evidence that these high hopes have been realised, except perhaps in Italy which has seen a proliferation of independent radical radio and T.V. stations, initially outside the law. A recent report on that experience states that the radio station can be a kind of 'tom, tom, of the collective subject'. The latter is regarded very much in working class terms. Comparing this experience with 'community' experiments in England and U.S.A., the report concludes that 'the concept of community is foreign to Italian thinking. In other countries the point of departure for alternative communications is very often the community taken in its widest sense, but in Italy the point of reference is always the working class, or the school or the district or the nation as a whole'.[8] Thus local radio in Italy has been used as a means of political mobilisation, as a service to radical movements of workers and students.

In Great Britain and U.S.A., the experience has been more prosaic, less grounded in class analysis, reflecting the diversity of views about community action and education discussed in previous chapters. As a result community media means many things to many people, e.g. access programmes for minority groups; community service programmes designed to encourage volunteer recruitment; a resource for various local problems and issues; 'phone in' programmes on personal issues and problems.[9] Raymond Williams has pointed out that, far from such initiatives presenting opportunities for community control of T.V. and radio, they can be a smokescreen for greater interference and control by national and multi-national institutions.[10] The only instances of real community control are normally to be found in local video experiments which suffer competition from, and comparison with, the larger regional and national networks.

In such circumstances it is less important to debate the relative merits of 'local' as compared to 'community' media than it is to decide who actually initiates a given programme, who researches and produces it, who operates the recording equipment, who takes the editing decisions, who accepts responsibility for the transmitted content. Answers to these questions are also more important than debating whether to opt for professionals or amateurs in the production of 'community' programmes.

Educational broadcasting has, historically, provided opportunities to explore the problems involved in such issues, probably because it is marginal to the total broadcasting system! Thus a democratic partnership between, on the one hand, committed educators and broadcasters, and, on the other hand, parents, trade unionists, farmers, peasants, has proved successful in various parts of the world.[11] The latter provide the material and the social network for relevant education linked to social, trade union and community action whilst the former provide the expertise on media and educational techniques.

'What is happening to us?' - Community Radio and Education in Northern Ireland

Nowhere is the relationship between the community and the media of such vital importance; nowhere is the problem more difficult yet the crying need to explore that relationship more acute than here in Northern Ireland. Discussion about cultural action, about community involvement in the media takes on a heightened perspective when applied to the situation here. On the surface the possibilities for the media to make some practical contribution to the problems and divisions, outlined in previous chapters, seems wide indeed.

This potential is summed up in a Council of Europe report about European experiments in 'cultural policy' designed to assist the growth of an informed and participative population by providing opportunities for community involvement in the arts and the media. It states that such involvement 'is not merely a new vehicle for self-expression in the sense of the arts, but also a great enlargement of the scope which people have for significant dialogue concerning their personal or social situation, for the constructive sharing of experience and, of even greater value perhaps, for that self unfolding which alleviates the dark areas which are inevitable in human life and for which men as sundered in time and place as Thomas Mann and the dramatist Webster have said there is no remedy save 'the avenging word 'and a true and understanding auditory' '.[12]

The C.A.R.E. project actively sought to use the media to encourage such a sharing of experiences, a self unfolding, about cultural change and cultural division in Northern Ireland. It attempted to create a democratic partnership with the media which offered working class people in Northern Ireland an opportunity to learn how to use it to speak to each other, to paint an oral picture, a montage, of their lives and to use this material for their own education in an informal, but structured, educational process.

An agreement with the B.B.C. in Northern Ireland resulted in a decision to provide air time, production assistance and editing facilities for such a community education project called 'What is Happening to Us?' over a period of three years. The C.A.R.E. project, in co-operation with local activists, was responsible for recording and scripting the material, assisting with the production and editing of the programmes, providing support material and organising local discussion groups. Thus it was possible to set up a partnership involving local groups and activists, the C.A.R.E. project and the B.B.C.

The experience of community action and education in Northern Ireland, particularly the experience in setting up local study groups, provided both the material - the themes for the programmes - and the network of contacts and participants necessary for the success of the exercise. Thus the initial series of eight fifteen minute programmes presented an arching theme, a general picture of the 'common' culture of Catholic and Protestant working class communities throughout the Province and the variety of issues and problems facing them as a result of social and cultural change. Under the heading of 'Family and Community' it used the voices of the people to relate memories, experiences, views, and opinions about community life in Northern Ireland, Protestant and Catholic, past and present. It attempted to illuminate the moral issues and dilemmas behind the 'cultural' revolution. As indicated above this has normally been seen as the province of the women's movement. However the cultural and moral revolution *is* part of the process of social and economic change, one which has deeply undermined traditional working class values and attitudes, particularly those *collective* values which traditionally stood in opposition to the individualist philosophy of modern capitalism. The crisis in working class life which that conflict of values has produced is normally absent from much community action and education.

The process of recording material on this broad fan-like theme became an educational experience in itself for all those involved in it. Recording sessions in homes, clubs, pubs, community centres, throughout Northern Ireland often resulted in animated discussion amongst the participants long after the recording session had ended! A door was opened into a range of issues and problems that people were only too eager to discuss. Thus, although problems to do with poverty and the general lack of resources in working class communities figured prominently in people's comments, there was also a great deal about relationships between the sexes, the role of women, the changing nature of family life, changes in moral attitudes and behaviour, the conflict between parents and children, the move towards a more individualistic approach to social and moral issues. This is obviously producing tremendous conflicts and tensions, especially in those working class communities which are also suffering severely from social and economic deprivation and communal conflict. It is no wonder people talk of a vast nervous breakdown at community level in Ulster!

The still strong oral tradition in both communities succeeded in painting a vivid picture of community life and of that 'breakdown'; of problems in home and community, work and leisure, politics and religion. People were able to express themselves, to put it in their own words, in a rich and colourful manner which belied their own lack of confidence in their ability to communicate. This was particularly true of the older generation who felt most keenly the changes in family and community life.

'My memories of childhood, coming home from school, was the big fire in the hearth. The fireplaces then, you had to black-lead them and you had to use emery paper on the stainless steel that was round them. You had the brasses gleaming on the fireplaces, plaques up round the walls were also gleaming. We had a wee shop and my mother used to send us (my sister and I) for the barrels of apples. Now they weren't very big barrels of apples, because we were able to carry them between us. She would have made candy apples and the people of the street would have come round that there would have been a couple waiting on my mother's candy apples. The potato bread, I remember her, she used to bake and that was practically every day. The soda farls sitting at an angle on the griddle and the smell from it was absolutely marvellous coming through the door. A few of our friends would have been there and the butter would have been melting on the hot potato bread and running down our fingers. We would have been eating up the potato bread and licking our fingers. The backs of our hands would be covered with the melted butter which was absolutely fabulous when you think of it.

'The warmth and pleasure of that small house will never be erased from my memory because of the happiness of it, the warmth of it. It was a haven. It was somewhere to go. And the people in it, the love that was there it comes back down through the generations . . . . When you think of the street you lived in, the neighbours were neighbours, if you get the meaning. If there was hardship, the good times were shared, the hardship was shared. It didn't just mean that a neighbour was able to come in and talk about their hard times. If you had something you would give it to a neighbour to make life a little bit easier for them. That was the companionship and the neighbourliness that existed. It does not exist now because you have these large estates, you have the width of the streets first and foremost which divide the neighbour from the far side of the street. Things are so materialistic now. Everyone has to own a car, they have to own a colour T.V. and they have to have a telephone. It's 'I have to have'. It's not a case of needing a thing. It's just to have it to be better than the other person'.

That picture of the past confirms a comment Brian Jackson made some time ago that 'working class language can have a peculiar power of uttering direct personal experience, not only through description and anecdote .... but through image and metaphor like the great creative artist'.[13]   Radio is a perfect medium for such creative abilities. However, the comments outlined above also vividly underlined a theme which was common amongst almost all the older working class generation interviewed when they compared the past with the present, i.e. a feeling that, despite all the changes for the better, something had gone wrong, something had been lost, something of value had been cast overboard.

It is too easy to put this down to old age and traditional working class sentimentality and nostalgia. This is to dismiss those concerned as people lacking in any ability to stand aside from their lives and experiences, to objectively judge the changes around them.   Such a view is paternalistic and deeply insulting. In fact the lady's comments vividly illustrate the change in working class community from one with a collective ethos to that of an individualistic consumerism which constantly came up in the series. This was coupled with a sense of bewilderment at the increasing complexity and centralisation in society. 'Today everything seems to be this idea of centralising. But when you centralise things it loses contact with the people and the churches and schools are supposed to be there to work with the people. Certain things you can centralise but other things as I say the schools, churches, you cannot isolate from the people. They must come back to the community'.

Linked to this dramatic change in the neighbourhood were changes in marriage and family life. One young housewife discussing the differences between her parents and married couples today said: 'Well the differences that I notice in my parents, my father always worked, therefore we were brought up by my mother. She had a certain amount of lee-way. She also disciplined us. She did everything. She fed and clothed and laid down the rules along the line and you rarely ever saw your father. However, if there was serious trouble in the family he became the ultimate disciplinarian. But basically it was the mother who was responsible for everything. And his attitude towards her was that she was sort of a mother also. He would refer to her as mother or mammy or something. I think it has changed now, the roles aren't so defined. The husband is probably expected to do more in the house, to take a more domestic view of his role'.

A comment from an older lady underlined the same point: 'My father was always a family man just like my husband. Only there was that wee bit of a difference. He really expected to be treated like the head of the family you know. There was always that wee bit of a gap, him being the boss. But with my husband now with my grown-up sons they can sit down and have a debate, an argument. At the time of my father, if you argued with him, it was a sign that you were disrespectful to him'.

That change in roles has produced problems for women and between parents and their children . . . . 'Well the sort of thing that's happening these days for instance a lot of women go out as much as men to socialise. Either they go to pubs or they go to dances. When I was a young girl my mother nor anybody of her age group would ever consider going to a pub for a drink. In fact when I look back on my childhood, the neighbourhood that I lived in, any freedom that was going was the prerogative of the men. Women were very much confined to child-bearing and child-rearing and staying in their homes and doing what was expected of them. I suppose it's a good thing that women have got more freedom than they had in those days. But with that freedom has come a whole string of problems. The problems even in the children are becoming more manifest. When the children were young you could sort of cope with ordinary problems then. But now our children are all teenagers and there are problems arising from their teenage years most of us parents don't know how to cope with. Youngsters are sort of rebelling these days against home authority. They are sort of rebelling against all authority. This is something we are not used to. It is something that I was never used to anyway. I was brought up in the atmosphere that I did what my parents told me. I respected the Church and it never would have occurred to me to even speak back to my school teacher. My children grow up and other young people are just not like that. They will answer you back. They will question the authority in their school. They will come and ask you things and we don't know how to answer them or to cope with their problems. The old thing of obedience to your parents is definitely becoming a thing of the past anyhow as far as I can see and it is leaving many parents desperately worried because you know when I was young the solution to the problem was to take the strap and to give them a good beating. But that doesn't seem to work any more now'.

Allied to this questioning of authority amongst the young in both communities was a move towards a more individualistic philosophy summed up by one young Derry Catholic: 'Well I think most young people today have their own individual philosophy. I mean some young Christian people tend to take some bits of the belief of their own particular church and reject some of the more traditional beliefs. But I think basically at the minute there is a trend towards more individual thinking. Basically young people at the present time are not much influenced by religious teaching about contraception. It is much more the older generation, the parental generation. Obviously because of the situation young people find themselves in, there is more sex before marriage. They don't have the same views as their parents had. They are not so traditionally based upon the Church's teaching'.

The above views and comments are broadly representative of the response from a wide range of young people and adults in Protestant and Catholic working class communities throughout the Province. They formed the basis of the eight fifteen minute broadcasts which attempted, by means of a montage of music and voices, to highlight these changes, comparing the past with the present, encouraging

92

people to ask 'What is happening to us and why?'. The series was complemented by some basic support material in the shape of a short booklet outlining the main theme of the series, some information about each programme, and some suggested questions for further discussion. A dozen discussion groups comprising over one hundred people were set up to listen to the programmes and their reaction was very favourable.

'I thought it was very useful because it related the things they could talk about which came home to them and they could all contribute. Nobody had any inhibitions or feelings that they would be saying something wrong. The experiences in the programme related very closely to their own lives and it couldn't have been better in that respect. The discussion was very lively. They went at it hammer and tongs for almost an hour. With a little bit of help it kept very much to the subject and aired it very fully. It helped people to think of the changes in life and stimulated them to even further thinking and I feel the good thing about it is that the eight topics relate very much and force people to think what is really happening to them'. The same person went on to comment that because of the breakdown in traditional community life and the general problems of isolation and lack of communication in his district in Belfast he thought such discussion groups were vitally important.

In another group in a Protestant working class area the reaction was very similar, underlying the common problems faced by both communities. A member of that group made this point in his response to the series. 'I think the Catholic people have suffered as much as the Protestants and I think we all want the same things now. That we all want to work, we all want to live in peace; we all want to bring up our children properly. We all want that now. You can see it more and more now every day. If I am talking to Roman Catholics they tell me that and I honestly believe them because whenever you are rearing a family and you look at your children and you say 'Good Good are they going to end up in Long Kesh?'.'

Arising out of the relative success of this initial series it was decided, in discussions with various social, youth and community groups, to look more closely at some of the problems and issues highlighted in the broadcasts, e.g. the problems of poverty and inequality, the role of women in Northern Ireland, the special problems facing young people, the divisions between Protestants and Catholics. In this way the fan-like theme of family and community was broken down into its component parts.

Thus over the three years of the project a further four series were produced (a total of thirty fifteen minute broadcasts) and a number of themes explored in co-operation with interested groups and organisations, e.g. a series on social problems - poverty, unemployment, vandalism, social facilities, etc., for the Community Education Forum; a series on the problems facing women in Northern Ireland for women's groups; a series on the problems facing young people in the Province for youth organisations. Finally a series was produced exploring, not the 'common ground', the similarities and the problems shared by both communities, but the important cultural differences between them, the stereotypes they had of themselves and of each other.

This whole community education initiative was thus concerned to underline the common culture shared by both communities and the common problems facing them and to encourage discussion and action on the latter. However it also attempted to encourage more frank discussion about cultural differences, about the forces *dividing* both communities. The necessity for open discussion of these divisions was strongly emphasised by one Catholic participant in the initial series: 'If you could have open discussion about the divisions and find out how to understand each other I think this would all change because if we don't get together there will be no democracy in Northern Ireland and there'll be no future in Northern Ireland. In fact there will be no future in Europe for Northern Ireland unless we understand each other and try to live together'.

REACTIONS

The response to the whole series over the three years was very good. Many groups emphasised the importance of the fact that the voices and experiences were familiar. 'They thought it was great. People all over the Province all had the same problems we got. They thought there was, you know, really great working class voices coming over. And the songs, they really enjoyed the songs. It brought reality to the programme, the different accents'.

'I think they were interesting because of the fact that you were interviewing normal everyday people. You hadn't a load of MP's or councillors sitting there and you asking them questions. It's just the normal people on the street that's being interviewed. The ones that have the actual problems that you're interviewing them about.'

In one women's group the discussion took over the formal business of the group! 'They'd actually taken over our meetings. What we had sort of planned was that people who were not involved in the group would go home and we would carry on with our meeting. We suddenly realised it was ten o'clock and we had to break up the discussion and say we would leave it there'.

'It's a great thing to have a programme like that because it brings all the problems out. And when the people's problems come out there's bound to be something done about it. Because it brings every individual problem out, poverty, transport, community centres, housing, gas prices, it brings all this into the limelight. It lets the people know how we live here'.

As a result of 'bringing it out into the limelight' views were altered and in some instances action was taken, as the reports from the various discussion leaders indicated:
'I asked them what would you like next you know? Where do you go from here? And they said they would like to hear more, or told how do you go about it. What can you do? Where do you start?'

'I found certainly that we brought people together and they were starting to discuss and then we were left with the problem. Like they were looking to me for the answer - saying what do we do? How do we join community groups?'

'It made them more community aware, some even politically aware. The impression I got was that they had learnt how to criticise and they are not afraid to criticise any more. There was one girl and when the parish priest came in she actually criticised him to his face. She said, that was it. You know he's not up here anymore as far as she's concerned. He's a man and if I have reason to criticise him, I'll criticise him.'.

This change in attitude and perception gave rise in some groups to increased self confidence and action. Thus, as a result of the series 'The Other Sort', on Protestants and Catholics, and the workshops arising out of it, one group of young people from both sides of the religious divide co-operated in the production of a T.V. documentary about their work together and their own efforts to bridge the sectarian divide. Another group involved in the series on Young People in Northern Ireland decided to carry out a survey of social and recreational facilities in their area. A group listening to the series 'Them and Us', on social problems, decided to set up their own W.E.A. branch to provide educational support for other groups in their community. A group of women involved in the series on Women in Northern Ireland decided to undertake a survey of day care facilities in their district. In another women's group the members, who before the series had not been particularly self-confident, surprised the discussion leader with their attitude. 'We aked them if another series is run would you organise a group in your street? They said they would and I was quite surprised at that'.

Finally when asked if the programme did anything other than encourage people to talk, one discussion leader replied 'It makes them think which some of the people don't usually do'.

These comments and reactions suggest that this experiment in community radio and education succeeded at a number of levels. One, it confirmed that it was possible for ordinary men and women to say their own word, to describe their lives and experiences in a vivid, imaginative manner, illustrating that the oral tradition was not dead. Two, it indicated that this approach - although in some respects brash, unsubtle and unrigorous - did succeed in breaking down the mystique of education, encouraging debate and discussion about real issues. Three, in many instances this process resulted in increased self-confidence. Finally in some groups joint action was taken as a result of the growth in awareness and self-confidence.

However it would be misleading to suggest that the experiment succeeded in encouraging large numbers to take part in this reflective educational process. The number of groups listening to any one of the five series rarely rose above fourteen for the whole Province - a maximum of 140 people for each series. Many of the community organisations involved in the project failed to establish an effective listening and discussion network. They lacked the educational expertise, the structured organisation, administration and experienced field workers common to more professional groups, like trade unionists or farmers. In the absence of any network of community educators success in organising discussion groups thus depended on the ability of the C.A.R.E. team to recruit interested local activists. It was the enthusiasm and commitment of the latter which helped to get many groups established. Those who were already interested in education and active in their own community were most effective in setting up groups, usually amongst those with whom they were already involved. What they lacked in educational skills they made up for in enthusiasm and commitment. Support material, advice and some in-service training were provided although the latter was not as extensive as it could have been.

A major problem in setting up discussion groups was the fixed times at which the programmes were broadcast. Given the informal structure which typified many groups the set time for the broadcasts proved too inflexible. Thus many group leaders suggested that tapes or cassettes of the programmes would be more useful, since they would provide that necessary degree of flexibility and adaptability. In fact numerous groups and individuals made use of tapes or cassettes of the programmes. As a result of this feedback the project decided to turn the radio programmes and support material into a permanent community education 'package' for use when, and where, people decided. Given the video and cassette revolution this is probably the most effective way in which this sort of material can be used for educational purposes.

CONCLUSION

As far as the broadcasting media in Northern Ireland is concerned this pilot experiment in community education indicated that it could play an important role in encouraging dialogue and discussion about the common problems and divisions facing the population here. The Annan Report on the Future of Broadcasting welcoming the B.B.C.'s intention to increase its educational output in Northern Ireland, stated that 'Here perhaps more than anywhere else, broadcasting - so frequently under attack - can do most to heal the divisions of the past and soften the conflicts of the present'.[14] Unfortunately there is little evidence to date that either the B.B.C. or U.T.V. have taken any major steps in that direction.

Yet the C.A.R.E. initiative - though small in terms of the resources and personnel at its disposal - confirmed the faith of the Annan Report on the role of educational broadcasting in Northern Ireland. It indicated that the media could become an important vehicle for the greater enlargement of the scope people have for significant dialogue concerning the personal, social and cultural and political problems they face in this torn and divided community.

NOTES

1. J. Smith, 'Hard Lines and Soft Options', in *Political Issues and Community Work*. Ed. Paul Curno, (Routledge and Kegan Paul, 1978).

2. R. Miliband, 'The Future of Socialism in England' in *Socialist Register, 1977*. (Merlin Press, London, 1977).

3. J. Perlman, 'Seven Voices from One Organisation. What does it mean?' (unpublished paper, University of Southern California, 1980), p. 25.

4. J. Simpson, *Towards Cultural Democracy*, (Council for Cultural Co-Operation, Council of Europe, Strasbourg, 1976), p. 36.

5. P. Freire, *Pedagogy of the Oppressed*, (Penguin, Harmondsworth, 1972), p. 83.

6. J. Berger, 'Millet and a Third World' in *New Society* 29/1/76.

7. See for example the following Council of Europe reports:

The place of Radio and T.V. in Area Socio-Cultural Animation by A.J. Kingsbury, 1973.

Community Control of Local Radio by Peter Lewis, 1976.

Alternative Kinds of Radio and T.V. by Patrice Flichy, 1981.

Local Radio in Britain by Peter Lewis, 1979.

Two-way radio and socio-cultural development, 1977.

8. R. Faemza, *The Radio Phenomenon in Italy*, (Council of Europe, Strasbourg, 1977), p. 20.

9. P. Lewis, *Whose Media?* (Consumers' Association, London, 1978).

10. Quoted in *Local Radio in Britain* op. cit.

11. See for example:-

T. Burrow, et al, 'An experiment in Local Radio' - a series for trade unionists in Great Britain - in *Adult Education*, Vol. 42, No. 2, July, 1969.

M. Conway-Piskorski, 'Give your child a change' a series for the parents of school leavers in Ireland, (Radio Telefis Eireann, Dublin, 1972).

B. Jones and T. Lovett, 'Living Today - An experiment in Local Radio - A series for local communities in Liverpool', (B.B.C. Publications, 1971).

R. Faris, *The Passionate Educators* - A series for farmers in Canada in 1930's, (Peter Murton, Toronto, 1975).

H.L. Hall and T. Dodds, 'Voices for Development: The Tanzanian National Radio Study Campaign' - a series in support of socialist development in Tanzania, (International Extension College Cambridge, 1974).

12. Simpson, *Towards Cultural Democracy*, p. 61.

13. B. Jackson, *Working Class Community*, (Penguin, Harmondsworth, 1972), p. 13.

14. *Report on the Future of Broadcasting*, (The Annan Report, H.M.S.O., 1977, para. 26.41, pp. 416-417.

Chapter 8

RESEARCH AND INFORMATION FOR COMMUNITY ACTION

Between 1978 and 1980, C.A.R.E. put together a modest research and information centre at Magee College. One member of the team took overall responsibility for it, but everyone contributed to it, compiling support material for the radio series, collecting reports from various parts of the world, responding to requests for information or advice and establishing useful contacts. There were three main aspects to this work: first, building up a small library in our largest vacant room, which was open to public consultation and usually attended by someone who could offer advice on reading material or sources of information; second, an evening class in local social research that ran on a regular basis for about a year; and third, specific research projects undertaken by C.A.R.E. staff and others. All these things were reasonably well integrated into the rest of C.A.R.E.'s work, with many of the same people participating in this side of things as well as the conference, radio series, courses, etc., and with topics for research being related to the problems faced by community activists.

Success, however, was limited on all three fronts. The centre was regularly used by a range of people from around Derry and appeared at the end to be secure as a resource within the Institute of Continuing Education. But its usefulness was constrained by its location within an academic institution which deterred many potential users; by the budget available for buying source books; and by the failure to establish sufficient contact with people who could have provided information from within state bodies or other institutions or advised us on specialist matters, including, particularly, sympathetic trade unionists and professionals. The evening class was thoroughly worthwhile, but dwindled in numbers instead of expanding and failed to train students in research methods. The specific research exercises were useful, but suffered again from relative isolation from potentially influential local people. Overall, some worthwhile exercises were carried out, with unknown long term consequences, but they did not achieve the kind of educational and political momentum that other centres have shown to be possible. To some extent, three years was not long enough to get this sort of thing off the ground.

Ultimately, the main users of the C.A.R.E. library were the students on the extra-mural course in Community Studies (discussed in the next chapter), other Institute students and some Derry community workers. The second and third of those groups confined themselves to books and reports specifically about community work and related issues, like housing, youth unemployment and transport planning. The extra-mural students, after much encouragement from C.A.R.E. staff, made considerable use of the history and novels sections. But the library room had a larger function: it acted as an additional haven or watering place for all sorts of people interested in pursuing community action, alternative politics and some community arts initiatives around the area. A few people dropped in all the time because it was a place where their efforts would be taken seriously and discussed (and possibly because they thought we could do with some company!). It tended to attract those who were either feeling their way towards a new political understanding or broadly socialists, rather than highly committed loyalists or republicans. That was the image that C.A.R.E. had acquired and it was a political strand that lacked such havens for debate. No one who approached the centre however, was excluded; those who advocated political positions with which we were wholly out of sympathy tended to know that and kept away.

The evening class in social research was launched in November 1978. Two people who worked for a more sophisticated, though still relatively new centre in Leeds,[1] were in the North to give some talks in Belfast, and a meeting was arranged with them in the new library-resource centre. One of them had lived in Belfast for some time and had written a book on the political economy of decline in a Protestant section of the city.[2] They spoke to an audience of about 40, giving an account of the emergence of their centre, the issues around which trade unionists and community workers had come together with mutual inquiries and interests, the management structure of the centre and the struggle for funds to run it. Both spoke with the vitality of people whose enthusiasm for a new venture was undiminished and they evoked a lively response. By the end of the meeting, many of the participants had agreed to help C.A.R.E. launch a similar facility in Derry. It would start with an evening class, or research group, which would explore sources of information, collect basic material about the area, build up useful contacts and generally pave the way for a publicly managed centre, producing its own regular bulletin for a network of activists and subscribers.

In the event, the commitment was not sustained. The evening class was as far as it got, although the opportunity remained for others to pursue it to a more productive conclusion. In Leeds, the centre had grown out of a comparable class which, over two years, had produced two reports on, respectively, the social and economic basis of the city, combining historical background with contemporary political economy and prospects. The tutor had decided that the only way to achieve a coherent foundation for subsequent research was to allow the class to select itself down to a group of committed socialists, most of whom already had at least a little research experience. The reports that they wrote were consequently cast in the framework of marxist political economy and caused a good number of ruffled feathers among the trades councils who had originally supported the class. Though hardly models of good economic analysis, they did have the virtue, rare in community action circles, of providing a coherent account of developments in the region. Something similar in Derry would have caused quite a stir.

But Northern Ireland is a very different place. A class that confined itself to marxists would have been on the small side and effectively excluded almost all Derry activists. Instead, attendance was left completely open and the objectives restrained to more modest inquiries. It was also apparent that we were starting pretty much from scratch; very little indeed had been published about Derry's economy and few of the class had any experience of social research or economics. Nevertheless, the team pressed ahead, digging up sources of information and establishing contacts. They gave talks to three local trades councils, circulated regular minutes almost in the form of a newsletter, visited libraries and collected published material. C.A.R.E., affiliated to the London-based Labour Research Department, which issued a weekly fact sheet on the U.K. economy, a monthly magazine and economic analyses of companies upon request. It also made contact with numerous other centres, government bodies and specialists, with specific inquiries.

Much of that activity was fruitful. Over the succeeding twelve months, the team unearthed quite a lot on local private industry, regional health circumstances and health service plans, health and safety in and out of work, the debt recovery procedures of the public housing authority, as well as its future proposals, the confidential codes that guide social security staff, the long-term effects of riot gas and a number of other matters. One of the students/group members devoted an enormous amount of time to collating material on different domestic heating options, in view of the imminent closure of the city's gas company. We had a good initial response from the trades councils, but little subsequent contribution. We received inquiries from individual trade unionists and community activists, most of which we either answered or passed on to suitable specialists. We introduced a few of the students to the facilities available at the Companies Registry and the Business and Science Seciton of a large public library (the nearest one was 75 miles away, in Belfast). We advertised ourselves in a Derry community newspaper. We also viewed about a dozen video tapes, held at the Institute, on subjects such as council house sales, alternative workers' plans for a multinational company, international competition in the clothing industry, different campaigns to resist redundancies and common health hazards at work and at home.

But we failed also to achieve some necessary goals. The class should have received more systematic tutoring in research methods and more vigorous discussion of alternative conceptual frameworks for interpreting material. The arrangements were left too haphazard for that. We did not manage to secure the level of active trade union support that was needed to ferret out information on enterprises within the immediate area and also to turn such research to positive effect in campaigns to protect people's interests. In fact, we remained isolated in general, failing to find an active public for what we were doing. That derived partly from a lack of direction that characterised the exercise and then turned back upon us as growing aimlessness. We introduced ourselves to some important sources and items of information, but did not manage to consolidate this into a rational flow of knowledge, let alone an active audience eager to pursue the implications of what we discovered. The project remained incoherent and academic in a bad sense.

Some more general research projects were completed. Both C.A.R.E. staff and students put together reports on aspects of Derry affairs. C.A.R.E. staff produced material on Irish labour history, the status of women in Northern Ireland, links between Protestants and Catholics in the early twentieth century, developments in European textiles and clothing industries and the city's unemployment problem. The extra-mural certificate students completed a number of research projects and the evening class students compiled a comprehensive folder on domestic heating. Finally, a social research student on a six-month placement from a British polytechnic produced a political and economic analysis of the history of Derry and the North West of Ulster.

With the handicaps of a small, under-financed regional capital and little past research to call upon, what was really needed was a series of first rate academic theses or research investigations of the area. The Institute could have promoted (and could still) a school of research to churn out such material and stimulate enthusiasm for the subject. There were a number of people around interested in doing that, but they lacked a spirited focus for their efforts (which were in themselves, in some cases, heroic). Like many remote provincial towns and cities, Derry lost a good number of potential intellectual leaders to big cities elsewhere. Something was needed to stem that flow. There had to be a lead of that kind to provide a foundation for less scholarly research and also to offset the cost of travelling long distances to dig up the material (there is more on Derry in Belfast, London and Dublin than in Derry itself).

In the meantime¨ it was possible for a spirit of inquiry about the area to be encouraged and for relatively untrained people to make a start at generalised narrative searches in their own areas, organis-ations and fields of interest. The radio series (described in the previous chapter) fell into that category, as did the certificate students' projects. A surprising amount of unknown material can be disinterred by such informal methods. There is a danger of self-confirming bias of the most blatant kind, but that can be controlled if the research is subjected to critical discussion in a context like the certificate class. Which brings us to the general question of lay participation in social research.

RESEARCH AND PARTICIPATION

A number of different groups of people have taken an interest in this question. Community groups have attempted things like surveys of local conditions or of opinion about official proposals and others have done extensive oral history projects.[3] The International Council for

Adult Education has been promoting, for the past five years or so, something called 'participatory research'. Information centres of various kinds have sprung up in Britain and elsewhere, attempting to provide a kind of civil service for the labour movement, to counter-balance official sources. And some social scientists have attempted to put themselves at the disposal of labour organisations for co-operative research exercises. Most of those activities are still at a fledgling stage and many are distinctly vulnerable to closure or collapse, but enough has passed already for some lessons to be drawn.

This is an interesting area, where research and adult education have a valuable opportunity for co-operation, but it is also open to misunderstanding. In particular, we need to be very careful before we attach philosophical labels to these co-operative ventures; the question of research methodologies and theoretical understanding is not as simple as some adult educators seem to think and sensible initiatives will be undermined if they are wrongly interpreted and generalised.

On the positive side, popular involvement in social research is not only important but, in at least one sense, indispensable. There are numerous reasons for its importance. First, there is an uncomplicated democratic demand: if so much social research is going on under the auspices of state and private corporations, it is high time the working class people who are being investigated acquired some control over it. At the moment, hardly anyone outside the active research process is even aware of what is happening, until an interviewer makes an approach. Under any definition, it would be more democratic if, for example, urban planning inquiries, military research and industrial location surveys were subject to active public scrutiny. And it would be better still if representatives of trade union branches and community groups were included, at the very least, in the design, supervision and analysis of such research, despite the dangers of political co-option in such arrangements.

Second, there are a great many things about their own circumstances that people do not know. It is a common mistake to imagine that the people who live or work somewhere know most about it. Plenty of disjointed events, anecdotes, connections are known about, but they usually have a very limited compass and are rarely collated in anything approaching a systematic fashion. What is presently a set of conversation pieces can become the basis for some revealing research, because the other side of this is that most community education students immediately latch on to inquiries that unravel the familiar and taken for granted. To investigate one's own circumstances and history can be an exciting and illuminating experience.

Third, much of this is easier to undertake than it often appears. Substantial amounts of material are already available and are only disguised by their inaccessibility to untrained investigation. A short introduction to library procedures, especially in reference libraries, can open up a cavern of information that people never knew existed. If that is supplemented by some simple primary research, initially just oral interviews with old people, those with special interests or responsibilities, etc., a remarkably full social history and introductory political economy can be constructed. It is an error to assume that research must mean questionnaires and statistics: those are not the best places to start, because it is easy to trip up on the technicalities and, in any case, they have a relatively short reach.

Fourth, undertaking this kind of research contains useful lessons in itself. A great deal of unforeseen information tends to emerge, both about the substantive topic and about the process of accounting for the world; who is involved in what, who makes a helpful ally, where the brick walls are encountered. The one obligatory proviso here is that careful tutorial assistance is required, because little published research can be taken at face value and critical understanding entails a familiarity with the theoretical options. Without that, it is easy for a novice to draw some wild conclusions.

Finally, for anyone seriously contemplating full democratic control over social affairs, there is no substitute for learning about the actual processes at work around us. In that respect, working class participation in social research is indispensable. A great deal of it will be secondary research, from published material. It will also entail some primary research, where existing investigations have employed inappropriate categories or methods. Nothing would be better than for trade unions and community groups to set their currently unemployed members to work on this essential operation, with adult educators in support.

As for what is already being done in this field, what is badly needed is a vocabulary for classifying the different, often irreconcilable approaches that have been adopted. Out of a well of discontent with state agency and academic social research has come a bundle of different complaints, of varying degrees of plausibility. A list would include the following: that numerical or quantitative research techniques offer too narrow an understanding of social reality; that talking to the people concerned would enrich the analysis; that research carried out by academics is an elitist exercise or, in similar vein, that the professionalism of social research is a form of theft; that surveys conducted by local residents or participants, instead of outsiders not personally affected by the problems or proposals under scrutiny, are more likely to give a truthful picture of the question at issue; that all social research is necessarily biased; that social researchers should consequently adopt an openly partisan approach; that conceptual frameworks should not be imposed upon a research field from without, but instead allowed to emerge from the exchanges of a research process that involves the subjects of the inquiry; that western science is being imposed upon the Third World as an instance of cultural imperialism; that social reality is not an objective, pre-existent entity, but is constructed inter-subjectively by the people involved; that communities which suffer from social problems should be allowed to define, analyse and solve them themselves; that research teams should incorporate all elements which have an interest in the situation to be examined; that so many socially important events and processes go on behind people's backs that popular democratic organisations need to develop their own research facilities just to keep in touch with what's going on.

All of these claims share some common premises: that research, the knowledge it generates and the action based upon such knowledge have become politically sensitive activities; that there is a lot going on that various kinds of people either don't know about or misunderstand; that powerful interests, including state institutions, use research findings to justify policies in a spurious manner; that scientific research and the people trained to undertake it are often socially estranged from the people whose affairs are being examined; and that people whose lives are being affected would like more control over the policies from which they frequently suffer. What these plausible assumptions have produced is a really mixed bag of criticisms, many of which fail to offer an alternative to what already takes place, although pretending to do so. There is plenty of scope for fruitful participation in social research by non-academic activists, but such participation can not evade the theoretical and technical problems confronting all social research. Some of the 'participatory' suggestions claim to be solutions to intellectual and political difficulties in a highly misleading way. Inadequate research methods and hostile or insensitive social policies are not a function of the personnel conducting the initial research; that can only be an issue of secondary importance and, if too much is expected of over-simplified 'alternatives', the true possibilities for more democratic research exercises will be lost. It is most important that we continually separate problems of research methods and problems of the purpose for which research is undertaken; though connected, they are definitely not the same thing, as some of the critics tend to assume.

COMMUNITY SELF SURVEYS

If we take the different sources of criticism one by one, it is clear that community 'self-surveys' do offer a number of potential benefits. For a start, they can counteract poorly conducted official research, as when a housing authority relies upon unreliable sources, like its office records, for a statement about the number of vacant houses or the average waiting time for major repairs; similarly, where a planning survey offers surreptitiously restricted options to respondents, asking only where a school should be moved to, not whether or not it should be moved. Locally conducted surveys, like mass meetings and forms of unofficial ballot can evidently be used to test the validity of official conclusions. They also offer an important bonus inasmuch as the survey can be used as an opportunity to gather support for a campaign to alter the relevant policies. At the same time, it needs to be remembered that members of the immediate community, be it residential area or work-place or interest group, are often ignorant of conditions amongst their own neighbours, so that a survey can help to convince local potential supporters that others amongst them suffer from grievances elsewhere said not to exist. In the longer run, such research exercises, together with things like community newspapers and video projects, can serve to remove a veil of unnecessary mystery that tends to surround and glamourise the productions of the knowledge industry. This can lead to more critical responses to powerful reports and publications and to a democratisation of the research process.

Perhaps the most imporatant benefit to derive from self-surveys in the widest sense is less a matter of the knowledge produced by the research than of the promotion of a sense of pride and inquisitiveness about the relevant area or institution. One of the crucial weaknesses of communities which suffer the disruptions and depredations of a class society is widespread demoralisation and cynicism. Many people try to resist that withdrawl into hopeless contempt, which often takes the form of an introverted derision of everything the community has not got. Willis has tried to show how working class school students, once streamed into failure, elaborate a form of self-respect by sneering at the values and achievements of the society which locks them out.[4] However proud and sophisticated this counter-culture becomes, it remains an expression of resignation and defeat. People who try to dissent from this pessimism, in favour of something which refuses class division, are easily undermined; as most activists know, it can be a lonely battle to pull against a tide of sarcasm and disinterest. Getting involved in a research project about one's area, especially if that is supplemented by some kind of group support, can revive flagging enthusiasm and raise the level of people's efforts, quite apart from the usefulness of the knowledge which such research can produce. Too often people feel incapable of any inquiry of that kind and have learned to accept that their concerns are not worthy of serious study. A research group or some form of self-survey can combat that submission.

However, such benefits do not always accrue; self-survey also has its dangers and weaknesses. First of all, many community activists start with a conviction that they already know the real answer to the question at issue and consequently incline towards research methods favourable to their predictions. That bias is not, of course, confined to the amateur researcher, and if the hunches, estimates, prejudices happen to coincide with reality, then valid results may proceed even from invalid procedures. But if the presumptions are wrong, either the survey and the organisation responsible for it will be discredited or policy may end up based upon assumptions as misleading as before. The unexamined judgement of all community activists can not be assumed to be correct, nor even superior to that of a remote government official. The fact that a local individual or organisation sets itself up as a representative of an area can be no kind of guarantee of knowledge or good sense. Immediate experience alone is a very unreliable teacher. In many cases, for example, the assessment of one activist differs from that of another, one local organisation from a neighbouring rival; recklessly partisan research will simply help one to prevail over another without any rational justification. Such abuse of supposedly rational methods of understanding is very damaging and can not be in the long term interests of any democratic movement. Research becomes simply a weapon of force, bearing no consistent relation to reality, thereby losing all its validity and encouraging the very cynicism that activists have to withstand.

Secondly, self-surveys often labour under an illusion that the obstacle to satisfactory policy is an official misunderstanding of the problems people face: hence, research can show that more, or something else, needs to be done. That this is frequently not the case should be obvious during a period of recession. It is an illusion stemming from either a naively consensual view of politics or from an abstractly moralistic approach. The first of those has been endlessly exposed in community politics, but the second is just as important. It is part of what Thompson identifies in the tradition following from Cobbett in the nineteenth century, reducing 'economic analysis to a polemic against the parasitism of vested interests'.[5] It is simply wrong to imagine that state power is wielded by people hostile to working class people; damaging policies do not issue from animosity or disinterest, but from failed general economic approaches and conflicting political interests. Very often the depth of social problems is well known nor is there a lack of desire to solve them; what there is is an inability to reach a solution within the accepted political framework. Empirical self-surveys have no bearing upon that.

What that points to is a need to aim some research of this kind, not at the community's internal conditions, but at those of the powerful institutions that define its existence. That implies quite different sorts of activities, often less obvious to the inexperienced researcher. Many of those influential goings-on are far less well known, even to elected representatives and state officials, than the problems of specific communities. Even to start exploring those affairs requires considerably more expertise than the basic door-to-door survey. This forms part of the rationale of the information centres we shall look at later.

'PARTICIPATORY' RESEARCH

The 'participatory research project', sponsored by the International Council for Adult Education (ICAE), has operated at a different level, mainly at one remove from direct empirical research. What its co-operators have tried to do, under the enthusiasm of people like Budd Hall, is to reach a better understanding of what it is that afflicts dominant research exercises and how they could be made to conform to the interests of the great mass of the populations in whose name they are carried out. It is intended as a practical re-evaluation of the philosophy of social science, with a strong desire to find adult educational opportunities within a revamped research process. Both that intention and the open manner with which Hall and others initiated it, declaring it 'a call for assistance',[6] are to be warmly applauded. To establish some kind of forum for discussion amongst researchers and adult educators, including those working in the southern hemisphere, is clearly a valuable thing. What was less promising was the first crop of statements to come out of the project. Despite their consistent generosity and openness, these exhibited, in the main, a cavalier disregard for 300 years of intense debate about scientific method, as though these were questions that burst into view in the 1960's. As a result, important issues are posed and tackled only in the most partial and inadequate manner and this sloppiness, if it continues, will spoil the potential of such a useful initiative.

The basic orientation of the project has been to link social research more successfully to economic and social development, with a special emphasis upon the Third World. Most of the contributors to the debate have appeared to share a belief in some kind of self-reliant development, in the Tanzanian mould, reflecting both Nyerere's christian socialism and many of the basic tenets of community development theory. In their search for 'alternative' research methods, meaning ones other than questionnaire surveys imposed upon passive peasants and workers by alien university graduates, using pre-digested categories and exclusive analytical facilities, most of the contributors have expressed enthusiasm for the recent forays into phenomenology and 'grounded theory'. A wide range of intellectual authorities have been cited in support of this attack upon empiricism, positivism, 'orthodox research', 'quantitative methods' and 'the scientific approach'. Much of this reflects American social scientists' attempts to deal with the problems of their positivistic tradition, without actually relinquishing positivism. It also exhibits a strong tendency towards cultural relativism and the attendant politics of Third World nationalism. These are poor sources for an effective understanding of why existing development programmes so often fail, what are the possibilities and limits of a research contribution and how to approach social inquiry. Some of the writers are clearly involved in interesting research exercises, but the conclusions they draw from them as general guidelines for procedure consistently misinterpret what is at stake and frequently remain incarcerated in the very empiricist tradition that they say they are rejecting.

At some stage, the different issues which these writers have conflated need to be separated out and dealt with systematically. There is already a large and readily available literature on these questions to which only reference can be made here.[7] Too many of the categories and concepts in the ICAE discussions are vague and confusing: 'a strictly orthodox research approach', 'standard social science research methods', 'the myth of objectivity in social science', 'qualitative as opposed to quantitative approaches', 'allowing the human world to speak directly to us', 'development of people and not of things', 'emergent research strategies', 'cultural dependency', 'radical transformation of social reality', 'one-way detached research', 'agreed improvement of situations', etc. Much of this sounds evasive, in an attempt to reconcile opposed beliefs. We need to be more specific, both about politics and about the philosophical issues, if we are to clarify anything.

At the same time, it is necessary to find the limits of the contribution that any kind of research can make. Research strategies alone will solve very few social problems; research is of secondary importance, its influence entirely circumscribed by the economic and political institutions responsible for policy. It is all very well for Swantz to insist upon the ordinary peasant's rights to participate in planning and implementing their own development in Tanzania, but if

Nyerere's whole strategy of minimal development aid and a form of market socialism based upon co-operatives is flawed, then those peasants will soon get fed up with such fruitless participation. The real issue is not 'one-way research', but the politics of T.A.N.U., both inside Tanzania and in its relations with the outside world.[8] Just exactly who benefits from participation in research about the detailed implementation of development strategies that drag the whole population into a wilderness, with very much less democracy than the state pretends? There is something disingenuous about that sort of 'two-way', bottom-up' research.

As always with nationalist analyses, much of this 'development' literature assumes that the object of political and economic progress is a whole nation, like Kenya or Tanzania or, for that matter, Poland or Ireland. That too simply muddles the problems; Third World countries, at least as much as O.E.C.D. ones, comprise stark inequalities and political conflicts of interest. If we are to promote Kenyan or Irish development, whose circumstances are we to improve? and in what respects? A socialist policy has to concentrate upon the needs of the industrial working class and peasants, with a view to eliminating class conflict altogether; it cannot ignore such divisions and simply promote existing economic institutions, controlled by urban capitalists and rural patriarchs (including village elders and other local leaders), nor can it condone the regional or local competition for resources implied in a simple model of self-reliance. It must promote universal solutions, which incorporate particular problems in a global strategy. Categories like national development obscure what is really going on within the relevant country and help existing power holders to consolidate their position. Social research exercises caught up in that dead-end serve to restrain advance, whatever their internal characteristics. One recent contributor to *Convergence* seems to believe that informal health education projects are what are needed by women beset by the most monstrous exploitation on a plantation in Guatemala, a country subjected to state terror and bestiality for the last 35 years. In a country where the poor are treated little better than pack animals, it seems extraordinary that any self-respecting community educator can come up with limp excuses like: 'With modest resources, rural people are capable of organising their own communication or non-formal education co-operatives. Information and education will not solve all the problems of rural development, but they can help families cope better with daily living; and without them, other rural development efforts stand little chance of durable success'.[9]

If we turn to the question centrally addressed in the I.C.A.E. debate, that of epistemologies and social research methods, we find considerable confusion. At bottom, some kind of phenomenology is being offered as a replacement for empiricism, but only in a vague, inconsistent manner. This is in line with a recent fashion in the sociology of education generally, and in much of the rest of social science, but is struggling with rather than contributing to it. That whole trend represents a modern re-run of the *Methodenstreit*, which was so influential in nineteenth century German sociology and which, in turn, echoed a long-standing debate about the differences between social and natural science.

At its worst, the I.C.A.E. contributions are replacing so-called detached or disinterested empiricism by nothing better than partisan empiricism. That is the effect of following Glaser and Strauss into 'grounded theory' and adding 'militant commitment'. Once the argument accepts the notion of 'developing the components of explanation from the data itself' and 'allowing the human world to speak directly to us', the whole debate about realism is lost; all we can rationally uncover are surface phenomena, leaving the rest either to ignorance or, more likely, illicit intrusions without explanation. The only way this kind of 'qualitative' methodology can have any coherence is by confining the research interests to questions which are capable of immediate, local solution.

In economics, contrary to T.A.N.U.'s proclamations, that leaves very little of consequence. But its scope can be expanded by a reversion to religious concerns, as Nyerere and the I.C.A.E. contributions repeatedly do: 'People can not be developed: they can only develop themselves. For while it is possible for an outsider to build a man's home, an outsider can not give the man pride and self-confidence in himself as a human being'.[10] If the priorities are spiritual, as in this case, then it is easier to understand the desire to withhold from peasants 'urbanised expectations',[11] and Hall's doubt about the need for national statistics (after all, he claims, China doesn't seem to need many!) and his statements like: 'Development is more and more seen as an awakening process, a process of tapping the creative forces of a much larger proportion of society, a liberating of more persons' efforts instead of a 'problem' to be solved by the planners and academicians from afar .... The fundamental question is, who has the right to create knowledge'.[12]

Most of this is pure moralism: the liberation of more and more people's efforts is not the problem, since efforts are wasted without a macro-economic strategy that can co-ordinate them successfully, which is precisely what is lacking; the notion of a 'right' to create knowledge is absurd unless it is qualified by some criteria distinguishing knowledge from error and allowing the construction of hierarchies of knowledge for the elaboration of theory; criteria, in other words, concerning the *ability* to create knowledge; and to hold that 'people can not be developed', is a rejection of the crucial determining role of education, at an individual level, and of macro-social change in human history - it is also, more importantly, false.

None of this is to imply that social science research cannot be improved. Much of it is deeply compromised by its paymasters and then has the intellectual dishonesty to claim immunity from responsibility in the empiricist illusion. Much of it is thoroughly uncertain about the validity of naturalism and interpretative approaches to social science. Much makes use of economic categories without in any way acknowledging or even appreciating the specific theoretical schools from which they derive and without which they are meaningless. As a result of these and other flaws, social research often intrudes upon the lives of politically weak sections of the population without either caring much about their circumstances or, more importantly, leading to any improvement.

At the same time, one expression of class division in a capitalist society is to exclude a large proportion of the population from academic training and resources. One response of the excluded population is to claim that their insights into social problems are as good as and usually better than those of the privileged researchers. If that implies that official social research is sometimes woefully wrong, either through poor execution or blatant bias in category selection and analysis, then no one can legitimately complain. If, on the other hand, it implies further that rational research procedures, including theoretical training, are irrelevant in the discovery of truth about social reality, then it can only be a most reactionary response to the politics of class conflict.

Reason and science are always on the side of the oppressed, however often they are abused; their universal precepts need to be assimilated and used by any progressive movement. And that means that there can be no premature dissolution of the division between trained researchers and lay participants. There is plenty of scope of co-operation and intensive discussion, but the social scientist has a responsibility to perfect his or her craft and to contribute his or her theoretical insights into the debate. To arrive on the scene empty-handed is to mystify the whole process (in a way that parallels Nyerere's pseudo-socialism and the evasions of the Chinese Communist Party).

The most important problems facing working class people arise from economic and political sources and can only be solved by economic and political means. Research that can contribute to such a solution can only come from inquiries planned according to theoretically guided speculation. To collect data in a so-called 'random' fashion, however co-operative the research team, and then imagine concept formation occuring 'spontaneously' in team discussions is to repeat the same self-delusion lying at the heart of empiricism, which 'alternative' research strategies are supposed to replace. Concept formation of any useful kind entails a conceptual vocabulary which cannot arise from 'experience', from data or from blank intuition, since all those elements are shaped by conceptual categories in the first place. Clarifying and advancing conceptual understanding can only be achieved by rigorous and unrelenting theoretical discussion, continually reviewing as much as possible of what has gone before. That is the cumulative and universally co-operative tradition of scientific inquiry, setting it apart from and above the irrational prejudices and mystical assertions that preceded it. However imperfect it has been, it is an indispensable foundation for all progressive social movements. Political advance will be seriously impeded if, despite common problems, each locality is to search for 'its own truth'. Details of implementation and application need to be considered at a particular level, but ultimate solutions are inconceivable without universal debates and prescriptions, relying upon common theoretical traditions. The alternative is simply retreat.

One important way in which skilled researchers have tried to construct co-operative relationships with working class organisations has been through research and information centres. Many of these, like the Coventry Workshop, emerged from the Home Office Community Development Projects when they were closed.[13] Others, like T.U.C.R.I.C. in Leeds and S.W.A.P.A.C. in South Wales, took their inspiration from C.D.P. and from the trades councils which chose to support such initiatives. These centres, through differing over details, have done three kinds of things: they have brought together a range of labour movement bodies, including trade union branches, shop stewards' committees, women's groups and community organisations, into a committee to manage the centre's activities; they have accumulated reference libraries and particular research files to provide a data bank on the political economy of their region, available for consultation, with trained staff ready to advise and conduct inquiries upon request, and further disseminated by means of regular bulletins and publications; and they have used the centres as a base for workers' education classes on a range of topics, often issues of political relevance.

None of these centres have achieved political miracles. However if they are to succeed it will be through a combination of functions. The key is to recognise that information alone is very little. It is the organised relationships that develop around the centre that are crucial. The participatory research writers are right to point to the importance of involving people in research and development projects, because the spin-offs of such co-operation are as useful as any knowledge that the research may generate. Where they are wrong is in elaborating the implications of that simple truth. The research and information centres have so far avoided the ICAE pitfalls, keeping faith with intellectual expertise, while continuing to adopt a stance of active co-operation with all those people and organisations who seem able to contribute to progressive social change. The detailed judgements remain vital, but that core of skilled training and political involvement must be the basis for researchers' participation in democratic social change.

NOTES

1. Ron Wiener and Ursula Huws, from the Trade Union and Community Resource and Information Centre (T.U.C.R.I.C.), which produces a quarterly bulletin, available from T.U.C.R.I.C., 6 Blenheim Terrace, Leeds 2.

2. R. Wiener, *The Rape and Plunder of the Shankill - Community Action: The Belfast Experience* (Farset Co-op Press, Belfast, 1981).

3. See the work of Centreprise, 136 Kingsland High Street, London.

4. Paul Willis, *Learning to Labour* (Saxon House, Farnborough, 1978).

5. E.P. Thompson, *The Making of the English Working Class* (Penguin, Harmondsworth, 1968), p. 832.

6. Budd Hall, 'Participatory research: an approach for change' *Convergence* Vol. VIII, No. 2, 1975, pp. 24-31, p. 24.

7.   For introductions to this, see Brian Fay, *Social Theory and Political Practice*;   Richard J. Bernstein, *The Restructuring of Social and Political Theory*;   Keat and Urry, *Social Theory as Science*;   Ted Benton, *Philosophical Foundations of the Three Sociologies*;   Geoffrey Hawthorn *Enlightenment and Despair*; the various works of Anthony Giddens;   and Roy Bhaskar, *A Realist Theory of Science*.

8.   Marja Liisa Swantz 'Research as an educational tool for development' *Convergence*, Vol. VIII, No. 2, 1975, pp. 44-53.

9.   R.D. Colle 'The Traditional Laundering Place as a Non-formal Health Education Setting' *Convergence*, Vol. X, No. 2, 1977, pp. 32-39.

10.   Nyerere, quoted at head of Budd Hall, *Creating Knowledge: Breaking the Monopoly*, Working Paper No. 1 (Participatory Research Project, 29, Prince Arthur, Toronto, Ontario, Canada M5R 1B2).

11.   Ibid., p. 1.

12.   Ibid., p. 3.

13.   Some of the 12 Community Development Projects, located in neighbourhoods of 'multiple deprivation' by the Home Office, in the first half of the 1970's produced reports which presented a careful argument to show that government policy offered no hope to such areas, calling for a socialist political and economic strategy instead. In particular, they rejected the notion that problems of 'deprivation' could be solved at a local level. See *Gilding the Ghetto* and *The Costs of Industrial Change* (available from Benwell Community Project, 85/87 Adelaide Terrace, Benwell, Newcastle-upon-Tyne, NE4 8BB).

Chapter 9

EDUCATION AND TRAINING FOR COMMUNITY ACTION

The C.A.R.E. project gained considerable experience in the provision of short courses and workshops designed to meet the immediate needs of community groups and community activists. However in line with its desire to reach the largest possible number of participants the project sought to establish close working relationships with other organisations or groups interested, or involved, in this form of adult education. The work with local radio was one such attempt. The other was with the Community Education Forum.

The project also sought to link together in one educational process, the practical, the intellectual and the cultural. Building on earlier experiences, this was attempted through the development of a two year part-time course in community studies specifically designed for community activists. Both the work with the Forum and the Community Studies course represented new initiatives in a relatively unchartered field, where decisions of principle and general direction had to be made from the outset. Such decisions, both tacit and overt, reveal some marked differences of approach, which provide a useful anchor for a discussion of the options available to educators proposing to embark upon this kind of work.

It will help to clarify some of the issues if we distinguish analytically two kinds of question that are raised: the first concerns matters of immediate approach to the task, teaching methods, resources, learning aids, informal curricula and facilities for students' social life; those are the procedures and technicalities of a programme. The second is about underlying assumptions and principles: the purpose of this kind of adult education, the object of education for working class students and activists, the kinds of knowledge that are deemed useful, the place of political disagreement, notions of choice, democracy, authority, relevance; what, in other words, is supposed to be striven for and by what means. Evidently the two levels cannot be divorced in practice. But, despite some overlap in this chapter we shall confine ourselves to the first of these. The larger question of purpose will be left to the final chapters. We start here with an account of the two programmes.

The Community Education Forum Linked Weekends

The Community Education Forum was set up by the Department of Education in Northern Ireland, as 'a working group . . . . to encourage co-operation and liaison between the community and educational institutions and in particular to examine the educational needs of the community, community groups and workers associated with those groups.'[1] The Forum comprised a representative from each of the local resource centres (those receiving statutory grant aid, not the para-military advice centres), from most of the higher education institutions and from other agencies concerned with community development, including the local authorities. The Department of Education appointed a chairperson and secretary and, along with the Department of Health and Social Services (D.H.S.S.), sent its own observer. It awarded a budget of £5,000 per annum for three years, to assist the Forum in its attempts to pursue its relatively open brief.

Given the nature of the Forum's membership it was inevitable that, eventually, it would become a form of co-option which would defuse any radical element in community education and action in the Province. However, initially there was some optimism that this could be avoided and that the Forum could become a major educational resource for community action. This optimism was later to prove unfounded. (The eventual position of the Forum was well summed up in its final report 'The Forum has been accused of being a non-political body, that it does not take a radical stand on various issues of the day. It does not, could not and should not'.[2]) Initially however those involved entered enthusiastically into a lengthy debate about the nature and hope of the Forum's programme.

Eventually it was decided to draw together the various skills and resources available in a three-fold programme, consisting of:

(a)   a series of radio discussion programmes on community problems, with community groups participating in the making of the series and the Forum offering tutorial and other assistance to prospective local discussion groups;

(b)   the organisation and co-ordination of educational services to cater for demands that arose from the radio discussions, where participants wished to pursue an interest further or were stimulated to seek previously unrequested courses, conferences, seminars, etc.;

(c)   a series of weekend workshops for experienced community workers, leading to a week-long summer school, with relative emphasis upon a broader analysis of community problems although relating that analysis to immediate practicalities.

With some discussion, that general outline was agreed as a working framework for the Forum's activities. An Organiser was appointed, at first voluntary, but later on a professional basis. Committees were established to oversee the implementation of the proposals, with the Organiser carrying out the bulk of the requisite tasks, using her local resource centre's facilities (phone, typists, duplicator, office space, etc.). With considerable liaison with the full Forum, a specific committee set about planning the weekend series.

The Forum was very much an umbrella body, an ad hoc alliance for the singular pupose of trying out co-operation in the provision of community education. It was composed of widely differing people and bodies, many of whom had never previously worked together. There were representatives of government bodies, loyalist community groups, republican community groups, academics, clerics, small business owners, socialists, nationalists, conservatives. They came from all parts of Northern Ireland, some of them two-hours drive or a full day's return public transport ride from the Forum meetings, predominantly held in Belfast. That dispersal, both geographic and political, inevitably had the effect of magnifying the informal mechanisms of the Forum, relative to the formal procedures, and stressing the need for a pragmatic consensus of views and opinions.

Any kind of education service, and particularly one without a well-grooved history to guide its work, can only be mounted by innumerable administrative decisions and arrangements. If the formal committees do not often meet and do not run into each other in the daily course of events, then informal decision-making must fill the gap; executive power must be delegated to the actual administrators. That would hardly need saying within an association whose members shared strong common aspirations. In a field like community work, riven with disagreements, and a place like Northern Ireland, where trust is objectively scarce, too large a gap between formal and informal policy arrangements is risky. Given that context, although there were some fierce disagreements, the outcome suffered from surprisingly few shaky decisions or recriminations. Concessions were made on all sides. Indeed, that very prerequisite of the Forum's working at all became the guiding maxim of its entire work: reconciliation between different community work interests in Northern Ireland, state and working class, protestant and catholic, populist and socialist, became the underlying object of the exercise. As the Chairperson put it at one of the early meetings: 'The essence of the scheme is to create new relationships between agencies'.[3]

One of the many implications of that foundation to the Forum's work, which coincided well with one particular view of community work, was that, crudely, form took precedence over content. As the linked weekends and other initiatives were planned, the prevailing assumption was that organisational arrangements were more important than any narrowly defined curriculum. To educate was to make space for learning, in the most propitious way; to let learning commence amongst participants by clearing away obstacles to such enlightenment, including hierarchies, sclerotic institutional settings and other stifling formalities. Spontaneity and mutuality were paramount. That implied, not only a specific view of community work, but a peculiar approach to education, to which we shall return below.

A number of decisions were taken as to how the weekends should be run. First, they should be held in different locations. Northern Ireland has a fair number of large country houses, priories and residential centres available to visiting groups. It was argued in committee that touring them would give the students a taste of what was available, for their future reference. The Organiser's end-of-series report gave more reasons:

> It was decided to have the weekends at various locations for several reasons: so that most people had a weekend convenient to home; to demonstrate that education can take place in various settings; to make people aware that conference centres exist through the Province; to bring education out of institutions.[4]

Second, each of the educational bodies represented on the Forum should take responsibility for mounting one of the weekends. This did not work out. In practice, the Organiser found herself responsible for most of the arrangements throughout the programme. Particular people volunteered, one weekend in advance (usually about 3 or 4 weeks), to organise some of the sessions at the next. But co-ordination of the whole and confirmation of the arrangements always lay with the Organiser, who called upon her closest colleagues to help out.

Third, the students should have maximum say in the shape and content of the programme. This was taken to imply (a) a closing of the gap between teachers and students, and (b) a need to keep everything open-ended, from one weekend to the next; the content of each weekend should, in principle, be determined by the participants at the previous one.

Fourth, that open-endedness should be structured a bit, to try to incorporate different kinds of interest. Initially, this involved three categories:

(i)   reflection upon current work and concerns, sharing of experience, discussion of disagreements;
(ii)   technical skills and information;
(iii) analysis and discussion of wider, long-term issues.

In committee, that classification was supplemented by:

(iv)   speakers on a theme of 'leadership' and
(v)   drawing participants into running the radio discussion programmes.

It was also suggested that (i) could be enhanced if the students were to keep work diaries for the period of the course. Although all this narrowed the open options a little, sections (i) to (iii) were left entirely open and would take up the majority of each weekend. The Chairperson personally arranged all the leadership sessions, sending psychologists from his Department of Social Administration at the New University of Ulster. The C.A.R.E. project took responsibility for the radio sessions.

Fifth, time should be set aside specifically for social events, entertainment and possibly films. That should be seen not merely as a matter of breaks between sessions, but should be carefully guarded for informal socialising and exchanging of views.

Lastly, the series should be advertised to all community groups, who would be asked to delegate participants and apply to their local authorities for the costs of accommodation, travel and any necessary materials, so that no student should have to pay. It was hoped that this would begin to establish a principle of local authority grants for students on such community education courses.

On that basis, the weekend programme went ahead from the autumn of 1978 until early summer 1979. There were five weekends proper, one overnight get-together (in much more cramped circumstances) and a five-day 'summer school' visit to a resource centre in Glasgow. Forty-one student applications were received and accepted, and the group slimmed down to between 20 and 30 for the rest of the series, although only 10 attended all five weekends.[5]

The student group was very varied, ranging in age from middle-teens to late-fifties, university graduates and unemployed teenagers, militant loyalists and republicans, marxists and conservatives, feminists and a nun, etc. A few had been to conferences before; the majority hadn't. Some had hardly ever got away on holiday and a number had rarely escaped their families. There were some antipathies, but usually enough space to deflate them. There was a lot of boisterous entertainment and, over the whole period, a good deal of cameraderie.

The course went pretty much as envisaged. Apart from the first weekend, where more time was spent sounding people out, an issue was taken up each time, from housing to poverty, unemployment and education. They were handled in various ways: a simulation game, a debate, an economist speaking. Three straightforward skills were introduced and practised: video, newspaper layout and interviewing techniques. Three talks were given on 'leadership', five sessions on the organising of local discussion groups to go with the radio series. There were numerous 'limbering up', self-introduction and group work exercises, all designed to tease out people's experiences and help the group to coalesce. There were a number of sessions where students presented their own work: a couple of visual displays, two video tapes and a few position papers which were read out and discussed. There were sesssions for people to talk about the diaries they had been keeping, although only a minority had done so and those were not submitted. There was a 'book box', donated by one of the library boards, from which some students borrowed. And at the end of each weekend, there was a session for people to comment upon the weekend and discuss the nature of the next.

Throughout all this, despite growing student participation in all aspects of the course, the Organiser presided over the general flow of events, checking here, jibing or encouraging someone there. The atmosphere as a whole very much reflected her approach to community work, which was in the laissez-faire or so-called 'non-directive' tradition, keeping everything in the vernacular, discouraging emphasis upon literacy or systematic thought, encouraging spontaneous self-expression, indulging it when it went against her views. The weekends were characterised by this vary particular kind of liberalism. There

117

were some famous drinking sessions, the creation of a great deal of good will and one or two disappointed customers as well. The Organiser liked to call academics, 'epidemics'. On the whole, those who shared her irreverence towards formal knowledge and enthusiasm for face-to-face caring as a solution to community problems got most out of the weekends. Those who wanted something different got less.

The series ended with a five-day trip to a resource centre in Govan, on Clydeside. The same pattern very much repeated itself there: talks on unemployment, housing and social services; visits to groups, housing estates and projects; a memorable trip to the theatre (for many, the first time) to see a play about the convict, Jimmy Boyle; some complaints about waiting around. The centre was one with a very mixed reputation both in Govan and in Glasgow. In particular, its employment initiatives (basically, trying to get unemployed industrial workers to start their own businesses) making it unpopular in some socialist circles.

After returning to Northern Ireland, the students on that trip met once more to put together a written report on it. They met, however, in a house with neither facilities nor space for writing and, as in the rest of the programme, with no provision made for those with writing difficulties. The resulting report was extremely uneven and difficult to read, like a scrapbook of random thoughts.

Extra-Mural Certificate in Community Studies
The year after the first Forum weekends, 1979-80, the C.A.R.E. project launched a Certificate in Community Studies. Another series of Forum weekends was run concurrently, with fewer students than before, but C.A.R.E. put most of its time into the new course.

It had taken $1\frac{1}{2}$ years to get the course accredited by the university, leaving the team no option but to start the first year of its two-year run in the last year of the project's grant. Official recognition was sought primarily in order to commit the university and the Institute to running the course after the C.A.R.E. project closed. It was also felt, although it was not intended to push the students towards full-time higher education after the completion of the Certificate, it would be no bad thing if they had some token of recognition after passing out. That decision entailed a prolonged negotiation with the university administration over course regulations. In particular, the team wanted to keep exam requirements to a minimum, not as a rejection of assessment per se, but because it seemed inappropriate to this introductory part-time course, whose students we expected to vary greatly in terms of academic training and practice. It was also the first extra-mural certificate in any subject that the university had admitted, so the project was opening a new door, with support from the Institute as a whole.

That period of rather irritating delay (knowing all the while that C.A.R.E. was unlikely to survive beyond 1980) gave the team time to think through the curriculum of such a course and, specifically, to reconsider its ideas in the light of the Forum weekends. There was no doubt that the project was addressing itself to more or less the same task, but it was equally clear that it wanted to approach it differently.

118

In both cases, the problem was how to provide educational support for those involved in community action and similar quasi-political activities. In what way or ways could education help them further and sharpen their endeavours? It had to be an education that supported a social movement, rather than the social mobility of individual students.

Some beliefs and assumptions were shared with the Forum, but not all. One marked difference was that C.A.R.E. saw community action as part of the history of the labour movement, part of the history of working class people trying to emancipate themselves from class domination. That implied some rather sterner and more elaborate political undertakings than those posed by the ideology of welfare group work. A second striking difference was that it felt a need for a more structured curriculum and more formally organised teaching than the weekends had attempted. This would not be at the expense of shared experience, but rather in tandem with it. Other differences will emerge below.

It was decided early on that the course would be based firmly at Magee, not so much geographically as institutionally. Despite strong doubts that frequently arose when the university bureaucracy threatened to paralyse the project's efforts by inflexibility, it was felt that the resources, both of C.A.R.E. and of the Institute, would be invaluable to such a course. C.A.R.E. had collected a small library of books, reports, newspapers and other material scarcely available elsewhere in the region. Beyond that, the project wanted to avail itself of Institute resources, such as the video and sound library, audio-visual equipment, graphic design facilities, main library and simple things like the coffee bar and properly furnished classrooms. It was interested in responding to requests for the same course elsewhere but would have looked for a similar setting in those places, not necessarily an academic institution, yet one where such resources and the back-up of technical staff were available. Our reasoning was simply that, despite the rigidities of bodies like universities, having their support was much better than having nothing at all, in the absence of anything better. The various conference centres visited by the Forum tended to offer board and lodging, a holiday setting and not much else. The team felt that a fixed, quiet, comfortable environment would, over the two years, be conducive to sustained study and commitment to the course.

The basic format for the course would be one evening session per week, lasting three hours, from 7 to 10. The regulations that were finally agreed with the university demanded of the students two pieces of written work, one in each year, and one examination at the end. The course curriculum would set out to provide three things. First, in common with the Forum weekends, it would offer an opportunity for students to share their experience, acquire new contacts and new bits of 'know-how'.[6] That would be done by setting aside the first hour of each session for precisely that purpose, sometimes just debating an issue of immediate concern to a student, sometimes taking specific common problems which they all faced and asking one or more students to present a short opening talk for discussion. These first hours were to take the form of an open-ended seminar with maximum student participation.

Second, the course would seek to provide a substantial body of knowledge about the processes underlying community problems and to stimulate a critical understanding of the principles at work. By moving progressively over the two years from the particular and familiar to the general and relatively abstract, it would present an introduction to social studies, organised around the twin themes of community problems and the history of the working class. This would be done in the final hour and a half of the session, after a coffee break, mainly by formal lecturers, including guest speakers, sometimes using films, video and sound tape. Lectures would leave time for discussion and would, where possible, use hand-outs and other material aids. Specific booklists would be recommended for each term of lectures, students being asked to read and submit a written review of at least one book each term.

Third, the course would aim to consolidate what was being learned from those two sections, to ensure that learning was cumulative and thoughtfully digested. It would do that by two means: (1) by requiring students to write an extended essay or short dissertation in each of the two years. The first would be a community study of either the area in which they worked or the group they worked for, giving background, original aims, actual developments, and prospects; the second, a research project on any subject related to the course that had grabbed their interest in the first year, possibly a deepening of part of their community study or anything from an examination of alcoholism to a review of nineteenth century novels of urban life. (2) It would consciously nurture an atmosphere of intellectual challenge and excitement, by no means sombre or supercilious, but confronting students with the pleasures of learning and the breadth of the intellectual neglect many of them had suffered in the formal school systems. To do that, it would start the first session with a 'return to study' video series, which offered encouragement on reading, consulting libraries, note-taking and ordering notes. The project would also assiduously promote book reading, recommending that students build up their own libraries and surrounding them with books at the college, history books, sociology books, books on economics, biographies and novels.

The syllabus was finalised in a fairly definite fashion. Practical 'workshop' sessions on relevant skills were a feature of every session preceding the more formal taught units, e.g. 'Community studies' introduced them to working class community structures, their origins, developments and prospects. 'Community organising' examined the U.S. and U.K. poverty programmes, other community work initiatives in Britain and Ireland and the history of such agencies in the North. 'Social and economic history' consisted largely of studies in labour history in Britain and Ireland. 'Skills seminars' provided a chance, at the beginning of the second year, for students to pursue further specific skills whose value had emerged from the workshop sessions and community studies in the first (not just technical skills, like poster design, printing, video, report writing, fund raising, etc., but also interests like Northern Ireland's housing, services for the aged, youth leadership, etc.). 'Social structure and policy' was an introductory social policy course, covering the history, functioning and current developments of the welfare state. 'Theories of social change' attempted to gather all this together into some kind of conceptual vocabulary explaining the principles underlying social change.

Twenty-five students eventually joined the course, some were already known to the team and to each other; more than half were not. There were statutory community workers, assistant social workers, voluntary youth leaders, nuns who ran an advice centre, members of a republican party (and advice centre), a member of a credit union (who worked in its office), tutors from a Youth Opportunities workshop and others. Previous academic training varied from higher education graduates to one or two who considered themselves almost illiterate.

The workshop sessions were initially taken up with people introducing themselves and their work to the group. Then they viewed a 'Return to Study' video programme for a few weeks. After that, hand-outs from Community Action magazine and the Community Projects Foundation were distributed to stimulate discussion on issues, like getting new members, helping them to join in, raising petitions, organising meetings, the value of a constitution, dealing with the state and with the media.

From the start, some people did a lot more talking than others. This made the team anxious for a while, but it soon emerged that most of the quiet ones could handle themselves well enough when they had something to say or genuinely preferred to reserve their comments for rare occasions. No one was left out of the coffee breaks and informal moments. It was quickly apparent that the course was a completely new experience for most of the class and absorbing for that reason. During that first term, the numbers did fall away until, by the middle of the second, the class had settled at 12 students, all of whom seemed determined to see it through.

Having set some preliminary writing tasks, in terms of book reviews, the team had to coax some students into knuckling down and doing them. This looked at first as though it might become a real problem. But, as the year progressed, one by one, that reluctance fell away, under pressure from both a growing enthusiasm for the reading material and, more importantly, the strong commitment that emerged to completing the requisite community study.

Those studies were, with one exception, hardly started before spring. Then students began to collect research material about the early histories of their areas or organisations. Once that first bridge was crossed, tutorial encouragement was all that was needed to keep them at it and pull them through to completion. Many surprised themselves with their ability to organise written material (some were already fluent in that respect). Different students found different members of the C.A.R.E. team most amenable to consultation and tutorial sessions were set up accordingly.

The studies ranged from the history of Shantallow, one of Derry's newer housing areas, to an eveluation of the progress of a government-funded workshop for unemployed youths, which merged into a highly charged debate going on within the workshop about the direction it was taking. The studies constantly fed into class discussions about students' current practice and political problems. The effort of putting together a short dissertation appeared automatically to stimulate careful re-examination of old issues, some of which had previously been closed.

As for the lectures, the first term, when the students were introduced to a number of published community studies, from Bethnal Green to Belfast's Shankill, seemed to arouse considerable interest. The second term flowed less well, because it was tied too much to specific books and projects, instead of synthesizing a wider range of material. Also, the first flush of student enthusiasm had faded by the second term, requiring good presentation to sustain their interest. The third term, however, produced the most positive reaction of all. The history lectures, particularly about the beginnings of the nineteenth century labour movement, held many of them spellbound. It was not only new material but seemed to clarify or unsettle many contemporary preoccupations. The only negative response was from a strongly nationalistic student, who felt that Protestant radicalism in Ireland was being exaggerated to prove a point against republican myths; but even that student seemed content to listen and argue a different case.

By the end of the year, this committed group of students were thoroughly involved in the course. The ones around Derry made regular visits to the C.A.R.E. offices, either for their dinner, or for some assistance or for a general chat. Some came because C.A.R.E. team members were involved with them in various campaigns; some even though they were not. The main worry was that the C.A.R.E. project would be disbanded, with the end of its grant, before the second year of the course started. In the event, though C.A.R.E. closed down, the course continued, with the help of other Institute staff, and all the students completed successfully, producing some excellent community studies.

Technique and Method
In the rest of this chapter we shall look briefly at questions of technique and resources, at the kinds of practicalities that arise in this sort of work and at some problems of pedagogy.

Student Selection
If it is evident that educational method must be related to the intentions of a course, it must also take account of the kind of students that are to be attracted to it. Such generic differences are less to do with congenital, or even achieved, academic abilities than with the aspirations students bring to their studies. Marginal areas of education confront a highly differentiated 'market'. In our context, it is not particularly helpful to speak of appealing to 'those involved in community action' or 'community activists' or claiming to know what 'community workers' want. The merest glance at community action reveals a hundred-and-one variations, to say nothing of the possibility

that some people who are not presently active might become so and that such disenchanted potential might be crucial to the enterprise.

We have to ask what kind of people from this diverse and shifting population we want to attract. Not to do so is an evasion, by a pretence of absolute consumer sovereignty. It is impossible to avoid attracting one set of people and deterring others, divided in terms of either educational aspirations, pure and simple, or political attitudes. It is not a question of excluding anyone from courses; it is simply a matter of deciding, for example, whether you want people who see intellectual training as necessary or important, or others who value some kind of sensitivity training much more highly. You can not cater simultaneously for people who want to pursue the study of social history or formal economics to an intensive level and others who consider literacy hardly relevant to community work, except by sacrificing one group's interest to the other's.

Most educators working in this field want, as did C.A.R.E., to set up exercises with and for people whose interests covered a wide range. In some cases, C.A.R.E. envisaged people moving through different kinds of education, from local radio discussion groups to weekend workshops to the extra-mural certificate (though not necessarily in that direction). The project also hoped that it could offer something worthwhile, at least in terms of resources, to people who wanted no more than a chance to say their piece about local facilities or a pressing social problem. What was learned was that the different sorts of exercises needed to be thought out carefully in terms of what was sought and what kind of students would benefit.

Location, facilities, resources

What you need, in the form of facilities, obviously depends on what you are going to do. What you do not need are tasks positively hindered by inappropriate resources. There are some educational exercises whose success is facilitated by space and simple surroundings. There are others that call for technology, both simple and sophisticated. It is unwise to run one of each in the same location. Specifically, the first needs to avoid fragile objects and the second often needs, not only adequate fittings, but also technical staff for maintenance support. To skimp on staff or resources in the latter case is a false economy, which simply diminishes the quality of the education.

Just as boisterous physical exercises are out of place in a sombre classroom, where people feel they are being watched, so intellectual tasks are virtually out of the question in noisy surroundings, subject to constant interruption, where there are no tables or desks upon which to write (or, alternatively, computer terminals to operate). The physical facilities and the educational requirements are easily mismatched and that can be especially demoralizing in the case of academically weak or shy students embarking on intellectual study. They need all the positive aids to learning that they can get.

Similarly, both the location and the general tone established by the organisers of a course can generate an atmosphere which attaches meanings to the physical resources available. Basic resources, rooms, tables, walls, etc., are not limited to a single function; the way an exercise is set up affects the mood in which they are approached and treated. That may be stating the obvious, but needs to be taken into account. For instance, students at both the weekends and the Magee course were given card folders containing hand-outs; in the case of the weekends, short reports on projects, students' pieces, small booklets, the odd summary from a book; on the certificate course, reading lists, course summaries, historical facsimiles, booklets, photocopies, etc. Two differences arose. First, at the weekends, the contents of the folder were scarcely mentioned during the weekend; students subsequently read much of the material and often remarked on its usefulness and occasionally something from it would form the agenda for one of the sessions. But overall the folder material was tangential to the course, like a bonus to take home, rather than central to it. On the certificate course, the hand-outs, though occasionally given in a bunch in advance, generally formed the material for each week's lecture or workshop session. There were other items sometimes, but they were exceptions. A different emphasis was being given to the written material in each case.

Secondly, in the Magee case, C.A.R.E. decided, on a hunch, to get some folders printed with a course logo on the outside and to do some matching letterheads for the hand-outs. Without any special confidence in this, the team wondered whether this wouldn't give the students a sense that the organisers had gone to some trouble to think the course through and prepare something coherent for them. Evidently, such packaging could equally conceal a lack of such preparation, but in this case we felt that not to be true. In the event, there seemed to be a sense of membership of the class and of prompting students that they had embarked on quite a long enterprise, somehow attaching to those folders, although we have no definite evidence to verify that. Interestingly, when similar graphic design assistance was suggested by one of the C.A.R.E. team during an acrimonious written debate within the Forum, one of the responses was hostile in the following form:

> Where would we get the designers to work with each of 29 participants across the Province and who would organise it and how would we pay for it? Even if we had achieved it what good would it have done? Community work is not moulded, slick and professional, it is alive and vibrant.[7]

The dichotomy proposed here, between 'slickness' and 'vitality', is not uncommon in community work. It is quite misleading: there is no reason why any of the views of community action should include hostility towards the skills of a graphic artist, unless the most backward-looking voluntary service is what is envisaged. Skilled visual presentation, indeed skilled presentation of any kind, need not overwhelm students with a sense of their own ignorance. On the contrary, it can raise aspirations towards practising and acquiring those same or comparable skills, particularly if the relevant artist is available as part of the teaching staff and students can witness the fabrication process. There is, nevertheless, ultimately a difference of principle here, about the proper attitude of education to refined and elaborate skills, posing, at its purest, simplicity against sophistication. That is an issue we shall return to later.

Active learning and variety of stimulation

Sitting in rows, on hard chairs, fidgetting to the sound of a lecturer droning on about some scarcely remembered subject is a bad experience. In the context of community education, where many students are feeling the water, uncertain whether education really has anything to offer them, it can be a critical experience, leading to final rejection. It can revive a load of nauseating memories of the blunt end of childhood socialisation, drifting off into fantasies through boredom, in danger of physical violence at the whim of an immature teacher, loathing every possible sensation aroused by the classroom. It is very important, in this field, to remember just how much people can hate school. Many of the disciplines of childhood are painful, even when necessary; learning to write, for example, very commonly coincides with being commanded to sit up straight in a chair and adopt dozens of other uncomfortable manners enforced by outsized humans who just happen to have the whip-hand.[8] Resentment of such confinements is a whole lot worse for people who early on get wise to their rejection by the school system, the millions of failures it consistently turns out. Many of the adults to whom community education is addressed have had that profoundly damaging experience and it has left an entrenched mistrust of all things school-like.

As if that were not enough, many of the same people have learned that engaging in public activities of any kind can entail the interminable meeting, as parodied by Tressell, whose house-painters open a meeting to decide on the location of the year's annual outing with the chair meandering on:

> Possibly with a laudable desire that there should be no mistake about it, he took the trouble to explain several times, going over the same ground and repeating the same words over and over again, whilst the audience waited in a deathlike and miserable silence for him to leave off. Payne, however, did not appear to have any intention of leaving off, for he continued, like a man in a trance, to repeat what he had said before, seeming to be under the impression that he had to make a separate explanation to each individual member of the audience. At last the crowd could stand it no longer, and began to shout, 'Hear, hear' and to bang bits of wood and hammers on the floor and the benches; and then, after a final repetition of the statement, that the object of the meeting was to consider the advisability of holding an outing, or beanfeast, the chairman collapsed on to a carpenter's stool and wiped the sweat from his forehead.[9]

Community education has to avoid that awful scene. Student vitality and interest has to be engaged and sustained, more even than with students of a conventional course where the prospect of individual

125

social mobility is a stong incentive to plough on. Community education can guarantee no such advancement.

Enthusiasm can be elicited in a number of ways. Best of all, the course becomes a pleasureable vocation, for which the student acquires a determination to learn and to push him- or herself on. All courses need to search for that kind of commitment but, in between times, there remains a problem of immediate attention. The basic requirements here are that students be called upon regularly to perform active tasks and that, in periods of relative physical passivity, their senses should be stimulated in a variety of ways.

The kind of active learning adopted depends, once again, upon the object in view. It can vary from physical sports (for adventure playground workers), to role plays (for group work trainees), to intellectual exercises (for more academic courses). The principle is the same: students need to have something asked to them, they need to produce, to offer something of themselves, as well as engaging more quietly with other performers. Learning is consolidated by practice, instead of slipping by, like a succession of glimpsed television programmes. Active engagement with ideas can transform listening into critical absorption. At the same time, sitting still, attending to distant actors, however inspired, is tiring if unrelieved by breaks involving something else. What theatre-goer has not found him- or herself nodding off occasionally at the most entrancing play?

Secondly, there is evidence to suggest that audience attention to a single source of stimulation has a limited threshold beyond which it falls away dramatically. This is lengthened primarily by appealing to more than one perceptual sense. Hence, a lecturer sitting still at a desk, with a minimum of expressive gestures and the misfortune of a dull voice, is likely to lose the audience after a maximum of about 20 minutes. Any kind of audio-visual supplements to that single source, from dramatic gestures and emphasis to a troupe of actors embodying the requisite message, can help to enhance student attention. This need not distract from even the most narrowly intellectual discipline.

It would appear, simply from the general experience of C.A.R.E.'s work, that this need for variety is pronounced among community education students.

Sensibilities

Finally in this section, a brief look at the question of skills. A lot is sometimes made of distinction between technical training in skills and education in matters of value, attitude and political judgement. In community action, that distinction is closely parallelled by one between skills and examination of the issues at stake. Without exploring this question at all thoroughly some scepticism is called for. C. Wright Mills had an interesting third category in his assessment of liberal education:

> I do not believe that skills and values can so easily be separated as in our search for the supposed neutrality of skills we sometimes assume . . . . Of course, there is a scale, with skills at one end and values at the other, but it is the middle range of this

scale, which I would call *sensibilities*, that should interest us most .... Alongside skill and value we ought to put sensibility, which includes them both and more besides: it includes a sort of therapy in the ancient sense of clarifying one's knowledge of one's self, it includes the imparting of all those skills of controversy with oneself which we call thinking, and with others which we call debate.[10]

Two things need to be said about this (regardless of whether or not we accept Mills' epistemological assumptions). First, the generally desirable objective, the nurturing of a certain sort of sensibility, can be missed on either side. Community action, indeed, working class politics as a whole, is prone to anti-intellectualism, to overestimating the 'practical', the 'down-to-earth' technicalities of a field of inquiry and pooh-poohing 'theory' as a luxury or an irrelevance. We shall look further at this later, as part of the question of 'relevance'. But it is worth saying here that all human skills are practised within the context of a superior, social purpose, with larger strategic plans at work. Such purposes and strategies will inevitably be discussed and implemented or pursued by someone. Any education that purports to enlarge the autonomy of its students, as does virtually all community education, can not consistently teach skills and neglect the social context within which they are practised. That standard separates an able robot from an accomplished human being. However, the converse error is not uncommon. The 'values', 'attitudes', etc., that people must adopt in their lives can only be discussed in total abstraction from technical demands and information at the expense of all intelligibility. Especially when we are concerned with people active in social and political enterprises, the possession of sharpened sets of personal values or an elaborate catechism is useless if the practical implications of such principles are insufficiently examined. In fact, in politics it is worse than that, since any politician will mouth worthy intentions (who isn't in favour of eliminating poverty, unemployment, war, etc?); empty rhetoric is the elixir of shabby politics and guaranteed to magnify the cynicism of already despondent publics.

Secondly, in reality, such one-sided educational approaches are more properly seen as delusions, since it is impossible to focus exclusively on one side or other of that divide. There is no such thing as purely technical training, nor a pristine examination of values. Each is an exercise in self-deception. Not only are the two inextricably entwined, but Mill's third, neglected creature is also an unavoidable by-product, in some form or other. The question is not whether or not we want to engender some kind of sensibility; it is, what kind? (What criteria for adequate thinking? What paradigm for debate? People animated by what kind of desires? Their strivings disciplined by what structures?) There is also the matter of whether or not we want to have it discussed, whether or not its rather cumbersome presence is to be acknowledged. In some circles, it is not a welcome question to ask what kind of person a set of educators is trying to turn out. To ban the question, however, does not excuse educators from shaping the sensibilities of their graduates.

By now, we are well into the larger debate about the purpose of this kind of education.

NOTES

1. Northern Ireland Department of Education circular, August, 1977.

2. Community Education Forum, Final Report (Belfast, 1981) p. 16.

3. Consequence No. 1, in the Organiser's 'Report on the First Year's Work of the C.E.F.', reads: "It has been demonstrated that co-operation between statutory, academic and community interests is a realistic concept".

4. C.E.F. 'Report on Programme of Linked Weekends'.

5. According to the Organiser's record: "35 people attended the first weekend. After the first weekend eleven people dropped out having attended only once which left 28 people who were committed to the training programme. Of these, 10 attended 5 weekends, 9 attended 4 weekends, 6 attended 3 weekends and 3 attended only twice". Ibid.

6. For an unexceptionable account of the distinction between knack or know-how or rules of thumb and a grasp of underlying principles via the development of an adequate conceptual scheme, see R.S. Peters (ed.) *The Concept of Education* (Routledge and Kegan Paul, London, 1967), Peters' own article, 'What is an educational process?' (pp. 1-23).

7. 'A Reply to Chris Clarke's paper' (C.E.F., June 1979) p. 5.

8. See H.M. Enzensberger, *Raids and Reconstructions* (Pluto Press, London, 1976) 'Constitutents of a Theory of the Media' (pp. 20-53) esp. pp. 47-8. Enzensberger's remarks are overstated insofar as they are hostile to socialising discipline of almost any kind. But they still have considerable force.

9. Robert Tressell, *The Ragged Trousered Philanthropists* (Panther, London, 1965) p. 374.

10. C.W. Mills, *Power, Politics and People* collected essays, edited by I.L. Horowitz (O.U.P., New York, 1963); 'Mass Society and Liberal Education' (pp. 353-373) p. 369.

Chapter 10

COMMUNITY EDUCATION AND THE WORKING CLASS

The C.A.R.E. project set itself the task of exploring options in the education of people engaged in community action and associated social or political activities, and also more widely amongst the working class population as a whole. With some specific areas of focus, this composes the agenda for community education generally. Baldly, what should educators do with working class adults? C.A.R.E. refined that nearer to: if community action is some kind of social movement, what place can education have in and around such a movement?

Questions of that kind are irrevocably political and consequently subject to some starkly irreconcilable answers. The differences begin at the assumptions upon which answers are constructed. Nothing can alter that. All we would make plain here is a reiteration that C.A.R.E. was inclined to seek socialist answers. Further than that, numerous questions remained unanswered.

These final chapters will concentrate upon a selection of themes that appear to run through all discussions of the subject: authority, knowledge, choice, relevance, democracy, purpose. Such categories can be used to anchor examination of questions about teacher-student relations, class-based knowledge, and curricula, 'really useful knowledge', learning by doing, sharing experience, the search for personal development, education of the will, instruction, discipline, exertion and assessment. Judgements on all those issues can only be based on beliefs about the kind of future society that is desirable and the best means of achieving it. The disagreements here are much larger than many community educators seem to imagine.

Background of discontent
To begin with, we have to locate these debates within a context of widespread disorientation. Archbishop Lefebvre, a Free Presbyterian minister, an Iranian mullah and a Hindu mystic may all rest comfortably on certainties about right living, right knowledge and the way to inculcate both, but few of the rest of us inhabit such cosy, tautological systems of belief. The developed countries of the capitalist west have experienced profound and vigorous disquiet about social and educational progress over the last few years. Massive social and political changes, innumerable generalised threats and unresolved

economic insecurity have combined to unnerve many previous certainties.

From the mid-1960's onwards, as the post-War boom ended, widespread uneasiness, both about accepted aspirations of society and the means used to pursue them, has repeatedly taken hold of sections of the population. What had been, for at least 20 years, reasonable confidence in the bounty of western scientific and social progress slipped steadily into anxiety about numerous aspects of the enterprise. Capitalist economics came under scrutiny from renewed interest in both marxism and environmentalism (both straightforwardly religious or naturalistic and as a secular concern about ecological damage). The dominance of European and American global interests was increasingly seen as imperialism and was met by a surge of nationalist politics, both in the poorest countries and in the heartlands of prosperity. The western scientific tradition, in terms of both empirical inquiry and technological application, was subject to widespread commercial and political exploitation and confronted by a revival of religion and mysticism. The associated liberal tradition of education came under attack from progressivism, relativism and varieties of anarchism, as well as attempts to reimpose reactionary dogma.

In all these and other aspects, publicly active people were seeking new methods of resolving social problems. There was a great deal of debunking old traditions, from the marxist to the conservative, and a search for new beginnings which would avoid the blemishes of the past. Although a platitude, it is probably true to say that periods of extensive scepticism like that give rise to progressive social changes. But what is also undoubtedly the case is that a great deal of indiscriminate carping passes itself off as progressive thought. Discontent and vituperation draw together people with quite irreconcilable aspirations. The essential thing is that we are able to distinguish the actual implications of the very different sorts of proposals that are on offer.

In community education, such stakes are relatively high, because educators face an additional form of contempt; many of their potential students have been abused by the formal schooling system. If education means school-as-we-have-known-it, then it can go to hell; ergo, education has to mean something different. That leaves a very open field. It is the answer to that question, different in what way? that really matters.

Some forms of 'alternative' education have assaulted the tradition of liberal schooling with a very blunt instrument. It would be better to clarify what exactly is damaging about it and what deserves our respect. We can not, for example, assume that what students dislike is necessarily undesirable; nor, equally, that what adult students say they want is an adequate basis for a curriculum. It is not a useful answer to private industrialists' complaints about schools failing to train people for the demands and hierarchies of industry simply to turn our backs upon the relationship between education and necessary production. There has to be some sober discrimination on all these questions.

Social class and modern society

Societies sustained by developed industrial economies possess two characteristics crucial to the debate; first, they are party to a colossal network of international co-operation, trade and inter-dependence, covering innumerable human interests, from some thousands of raw materials to a cumulative (and irreversible) exchange of knowledge, research and information; second, they are character-ised by profound divisions of social class, with subordinate classes separated by a chasm from the instruments and techniques required to manage such a vast and delicate enterprise. How we evaluate those two features of modern society is central to our judgement of the purpose of adult and community education. To oversimplify, is the first either desirable or replaceable? and is the second inevitable or capable of elimination? in the short-, medium- or long-term? Everyone in working class adult education has to answer such questions, even if only in effect.

Much attention is given to the second of those two character-istics, with attitudes to class division a major criterion for political disagreement. But the first factor is at least as important. How we assess the past and envisage the future of what amounts to an intricate, international division of labour, effectively distinguishes some incompatible approaches to public affairs, even amongst people who ascribe themselves to similar areas of the usual political spectrum.

The development of an integrated economic and social system, inextricable from a complicated fabric of global exchanges, is part of a predominantly European tradition of secular rationalism in phil-osophy and capitalist production in economics. The origins of that tradition, as well as its peculiarly European development, are a matter of considerable debate. What is clear is that, in the modern period, it has been promoted or enhanced by and through a number of specific social movements, including the Renaissance, the Reformation, the eighteenth century Enlightenment, the English and French Revolutions and, perhaps most dramatically of all, by the Industrial Revolution. By the end of the nineteenth century, what this set of social changes had done was to set the developed European economies upon a wholly different trajectory from both their own rural antecedents and the agricultural societies of the rest of the world. The social conditions of production were completely transformed, including a trend towards more and more complicated internationalisation. Living conditions were turned inside out, as people moved to new cities, lost almost all connection with food production and began to travel in a previously unimaginable way. Technology, applied science and research experien-ced a renaissance of their own. And, not the least of the changes, there was a population explosion which continues to this day.

Coupled with the political revolutions that gave the commercial, entrepreneurial and professional class effective control over the major social institutions, these remarkable events gave birth to what can legitimately be called a modern kind of society, which has since penetrated most of the rest of the world, with variable results. Nineteenth century Europe was, and many other places in the

131

twentieth century have been, haunted by the question of whether such monstrous social changes were reversible. Both radicals and reactionaries have been so appalled by the costs of modern social development that they have longed for an alternative. But not everyone has reacted in that way. The founding fathers of sociology (a subject whose nineteenth century development was centrally concerned with this very problem), Marx, Weber and Durkheim, whatever else they disagreed about, were united in seeing the arrival of a modern industrial order as both irrevocable and, at least potentially, progressive (with important qualifications in the case of Weber[1]). The important question for them was how to deal with this new order, how to guide the new trajectory away from the obvious suffering it caused and towards a realisation of its vast potential.

Today the same dispute remains. Is the present, gigantic industrial apparatus really necessary or desirable? Can we have a different kind of social order, whose technology is simpler and whose exchanges are more commonly face-to-face? How else can future generations escape the awesome perils of technologies which seem to be running ahead of all sensible human aspirations? If bourgeois or capitalist or liberal industrial society is sick in so many ways, even threatening all human existence, can there be anything in it worthy of perpetuation or respect?

Education, being oriented towards the future, has to incorporate some kind of judgement on this question, even if it only amounts to a hedging of bets. Since a major part of the traditional curriculum of European schooling and higher education amounts to a veneration of post-medieval European social development and bodies of knowledge, from the natural sciences of Newton and Faraday to the literature of Shakespeare and Goethe, contemporary critics are immediately confronted with the problem. If the future is composed of local autonomies, a return to simple technology and a revaluation of necessary labour time, then most of the edifice of western rationalism and scientific sophistication is inappropriate. People classified as failures at school are substantially correct to identify car maintenance, carpentry and survival skills as useful, maths beyong an elementary level, French, computer science and English as useless rubbish. If, on the other hand, the future holds further rapid technological development, continued internationalisation of production, extended geographical mobility and accelerated scientific research, then the question becomes, who will receive the training required to administer this great machine? and what kind of education best prepares people to fulfil that task? In other words, the traditional agenda in educational philosophy and sociology is largely vindicated and much of the 'alternative' inquiry is going nowhere.

If we now link that debate with the question of class division and class conflict, we acquire a simple matrix of conflicting positions. If it is true, as by no means everyone accepts, that the subordinate classes in modern societies (i.e., the industrial working class, petty bourgeoisie, agricultural labourers and peasants) are systematically excluded from even a whiff of strategic social and economic management, then a judgement has to be made by educators of such sections of the population; is that exclusion either desirable or eradicable? If it is undesirable in broad terms, then can it be eliminated ever? in the foreseeable future? soon? The obvious point that has to be decided here is, what kind of place in the social order are our students destined to occupy or, for that matter, their immediate descendents, over whose education they are likely to have a lot of influence. If, as socialists and, indeed, all consistent democrats must argue, they should acquire much more influence over the society they inhabit relatively shortly, then we are thrown back upon the matter of what kind of society that is going to be. Only then can we discuss the shape of curricula with any critical sense.

Educational debates

The four-way matrix suggested above, if carefully thought through, is capable of generating innumerable positions on these issues. A look at the recent debates in educational sociology and at one particular theoretical opposition will narrow it down specifically to the kind of community education C.A.R.E. was attempting.

After 1945 (and the 1944 Education Act), British sociology of education was primarily concerned with the life chances of children with different social class origins. Would the welfare state, and particularly its educational arm, achieve its avowed aim of progressively undermining the privileges hitherto afforded the offspring of upper class parents? Would innate talent and habitual diligence be rewarded according to their merits, regardless of social origin? Would the tripartite secondary school system live up to its promise of granting 'parity of esteem' to grammar, modern and technical schools? Would, in other words 'equality of opportunity' be achieved, giving to all who sought it equal access to what education had to offer?

The simplest answer was that the reality fell short of the claims. The tripartite system was weighted heavily in favour of grammar schools. The 11-plus was, at best, an insensitive and inaccurate measure of people's potential ability and, at worst, a way of legitimating the advantage of upper class origin. Far too many children were simply abandoned as failures, when much greater intellectual stimulation could still be fruitfully given them and when the labour force still suffered from a shortage of adequately trained personnel.

By the 1960's, official public debate was shifting in favour of reform, in an attempt to make equality of opportunity a reality. Comprehensive secondary schooling, community schools and home-school links, informal teaching methods, including a more child-centred approach, and Educational Priority Areas were all parts of a concerted reappraisal of why a disproportionate number of working class children failed at school. There were two definite strands to those reforms and to the parallel developments in educational sociology: first, there was a desire genuinely to improve access to education for working class children; second, there was doubt about, and sometimes rejection of, both accepted curricula and the apparent demands of an advanced industrial economy. A prevalent theme in the late 1960's and 1970's amongst radical educators was the preferability of a general, social education over a highly competitive, repeatedly examined, arbitrarily disciplined schooling, whose syllabus paid no heed to the real needs of working class school-leavers and adults. A radical alternative should encourage a co-operative ethic, grant students more control, incorporate more 'learning-by-doing', abolish physical intimidation and prepare students for the world they would actually face upon leaving. Much of the traditional syllabus was seen as incongruous, if not a form of cultural imperialism, browbeating students with alien cultural values. Various notions of 'free schooling' and 'de-schooling' gained many adherents, most seeking a more 'authentic' educational experience for students, to replace the author-itarian impositions of conventional schooling. Many would have accepted A.S. Neill's basic axiom, that people will learn what they want to know if they are left alone. If teaching was required at all, it should take the form of what Weber called an 'arousing pedagogy', nurturing and drawing out the innate intelligence of the student, allowing him or her considerable rein to follow their nose and learn through largely unstructured discovery. Students would be given the opportunity to discover their own truths, instead of always having to take things on trust from some venerable authority.

This debate about policy was later paralleled in sociology, with a shift in the 1970's, from concern about access to education, to a focus upon phenomenology and the sociology of knowledge. Following the publication of Young's *Knowledge and Control* there developed a school of argument rejecting conventional curricula for imposing bourgeois values on lower class students and for exploiting schooling as a pretext for the inculcation of capitalist industrial relations and practices.[2]

As before, progressivism has not only incorporated numerous specific positions, but also united people identifying capitalism as the main destructive influence with others who blame modern industrial society, irrespective of the political arrangements that constitute it. Equally, defenders of the general structure of traditional schooling include wide political differences, here based more on the question of social class than on that of modern industrial production. Not all radicals in respect of class are progressives about education; nor do all educational progressives either acknowledge the existence of class conflict or admit the possibility of its elimination. All that can be agreed is that there is a great deal of disquiet on all three matters; modern productive methods, divisions of social class and desirable forms of education; and that such dissatisfaction is shared by people with little else in common.

One of the clearest ways of setting the parameters of this debate is to outline two paradigmatic resolutions of the problems. These derive from Ivan Illich and Antonio Gramsci, both committed to a radically new degree of human liberation and a much more effective libertarian education, but each conceiving that project in a markedly different way.

Illich and Gramsci

Illich's approach is supremely ambitious; he wants nothing less than a 'convivial' world, with all individual people free to pursue their own interests and reconciled with their conditions of existence. What is wrong with education at present is simply an example of what is wrong with society as a whole. It is run by dictatorial and rigid bureaucracies, insensitive to the supposed aims of their activity (e.g. learning) and committed to a disastrous social project: the pursuit of planned control over the world and limitless increase in the standard of living. His educational argument is fairly specific. Schools and learning are mutually incompatible; curricula and institutional settings are inimical to creative explorations of more or less any subject. Teaching or instruction is not necessary; it is normally inseparable from extraneous disciplines (making students obey authority throughout their lives, believe what great authorities say about specific subjects, etc.) and largely incidental to genuine learning on the part of the student. 'Most learning happens casually, and even most intentional learning is not the result of programmed instruction.'[3] Schools consequently fail to achieve even their alleged objectives, which are, in any case, undesirable. All they really do is pass on 'institutionalised values', make people dependent upon recognised authorities, deprive the rest of social life of its potential for learning and thereby sustain the human race's headlong dash towards a hell of ever-rising consumer demands[4]. That is the hidden curriculum of modern education.

The remedy for Illich involves restoring an educative character to the entirety of social life. People must recognise the possibilities for learning from all aspects of their existence and the circumstances that surround them. Their natural curiosity must be encouraged by developing an unending range of learning opportunities, available to anyone whenever they wish. The first part of this requires all institutions to abandon secrecy and throw open their doors, books, laboratories, accumulated experience to public inquiry. The second part is that learners and teachers should be free to choose and to establish learning networks, either in pairs or in larger groups, to discuss common interests and to pool what each participant has to offer in the way of knowledge. This would amount to a free market in knowledge, offering unrestrained choice to everyone interested and providing a setting in which individuals could match their curiosities with appropriate others. Such encounters could happen casually at first (Illich gives, as an example, a coffee shop where people sit with books and other items indicating what interests them, in order to attract others[5]), but would subsequently be open to more organised apprenticeships or co-operative research. Equally, some modern technology, like computers, could be applied to assist this matching process (convivial production of such machines is not specified).

Illich takes this free market notion to an extreme, acknowledging little distinction between children and adults and demanding the destruction of schooling for everybody. As far as children are concerned, he calls for a credit system, which would allow parents and, to some extent, children themselves, to choose educational assistance from whatever 'masters' or others they wished. (Unlike modern conservatives, Illich insists that distribution of such credits must be accompanied by the dissolution of the schools).

That educational theory is inextricable from Illich's general project, which entails, as he sees it, a rescuing of the human race from the 'Promethean fallacy'. That fallacy 'is the history of fading hope and rising expectations':

> To understand what this means we must rediscover the distinction between hope and expectation. Hope, in its strong sense, means trusting faith in the goodness of nature, while expectation, as I will use it here, means reliance on results which are planned and controlled by man. Hope centres on a person from whom we await a gift. Expectation looks forward to satisfaction from a predictable process which will provide what we have the right to claim. The Promethean ethos has now eclipsed hope. Survival of the human race depends on its rediscovery as a social force.

> To the primitive the world was governed by fate, fact and necessity. By stealing fire from the gods, Prometheus turned facts into problems, called necessity into question and defied fate. Classical man framed a civilized context for human perspective. He was aware that he could defy fate-nature-environment, but only at his own risk. Contemporary man goes further; he attempts to create the world in his image, to build a totally man-made environment, and then discovers that he can do so only on the condition of constantly remaking himself to fit it. We now must face the fact that man himself is at stake.

> The exhaustion and pollution of the earth's resources is, above all, the result of a corruption in man's self-image, of a regression in his consciousness. Some would like to speak about a mutation of collective consciousness which leads to a conception of man as an organism dependent not on nature and individuals, but rather on institutions. This institutionalisation of substantive values, this belief that a planned process of treatment ultimately gives results desired by the recipient, this consumer ethos, is at the heart of the Promethean fallacy.[6]

It is this general social theory, if it can be called that, which gives Illich's argument coherence. His is a romantic and strongly religious naturalism,* owing a great deal to Rousseau. 'Reality itself has become dependent on human decision'; 'reliance on institutional process has replaced dependence on personal good will.' There is no more 'tragic rebellion'. What are needed to defeat Prometheus and demolish the 'Myth of Unending Consumption' are attitudes like 'hopeful trust and classical irony' (much of Illich's argument is, indeed, ironic, rather than straightforwardly rational); 'a new sense of the

---

*   This is a moral naturalism, to be sharply distinguished from the scientific naturalism discussed in Chapter 8, on research.

finiteness of the Earth and a new nostalgia now can open man's eyes
....'

Illich poses his argument in a world where all important scarcities have been, at least potentially or as far as will ever be possible, overcome by existing technology. What remains is the question of how to pass the time thereby freed from necessary labour. We have to recover the virtue of 'acting' or 'doing' (*praxis*), as opposed to the art of 'making' (*poesis*); we have to end the frenetic struggle to dominate and manipulate nature and learn to live in harmony with the world, appreciating things and people for their own sake, instead of using them instrumentally, as means to an end.[7]

It is upon that political assumption that his educational proposals make sense. Learning in this field of vast opportunity can be come 'immeasurable re-creation',[8] instead of repetitive (and measured) assimilation. Completely free selection of single items of knowledge for discussion and examination by ad hoc groups can replace a syllabus of knowledge, organised in a curriculum, explored in stable classes over a long period, with instruction from specialist teachers.[9] Education and learning can literally become play. Necessity, compulsion, discipline, authority have no place in this post-scarcity, 'post-industrial' world, except where freely adopted by the learner. Illich has imagined a truly bountiful world, although neither his lament (the disenchantment of, essentially, the post-Renaissance world) nor his recommendations are especially new.

It would be hard to invent a more antithetical approach to these questions than that suggested by Gramsci. Gramsci's single most determined goal was to uphold the Promethean project, which he saw as threatened, compromised, vulnerable. The trouble with the world was precisely that reality had *not* become 'dependent on human decision' and the task for all social activities, especially politics and education, was to consummate that dependence. Expectations, particularly amongst peasants and the industrial working class, were too flimsy; fate needed to be wholeheartedly defied and 'man' comprehensively remade, in the form of an independent, sovereign species risen out of necessity, as far as possible, and reconciled with the world *on the basis of supreme control*. Prometheus' great gift needed to be revered and honed to perfection. That could only be done by showing respect for and carefully constructing institutions.

Where, for Illich, the character of a modern industrial society is the key to our present woes, for Gramsci, the obstacles to democracy were very much matters of class conflict. The universal inter-dependence implied by modern production, the expansion of applied science and the elaboration of larger human needs were all, for Gramsci, preconditions for freedom. The task was twofold: to secure the continued, if more sensitive, development of such productive forces and relations and to bring the subordinate social classes into a position of control over the whole enterprise. Education would be crucial to both achievements. Specifically, forms of education had to be constructed which would train the working class, not only for political revolution, but also, with equal importance, for the executive management of all aspects of the industrial order (from social services

137

and housing to international finance and scientific research). Political revolution would be both difficult to achieve and doomed to disintegrate if its preparation were not accompanied by the development of a disciplined and well-informed new ruling class. All other routes towards social change left the existing ruling groups in the inviolable position of being the only people capable of preventing social and economic collapse. Nationalism, communitarianism and anarchism all assumed away the very thing that made political and economic authority necessary: the continued existence of scarcity. The human race remained far short of the blissful state of abundance which would obviate the need for such executive and administrative acumen. Discipline, order, structure, stable institutions, far from being intrinsically oppressive, were indispensable for any sort of liberating social development. What was currently undesirable about them was the purpose to which they were devoted.[10]

With assumptions so markedly different from those of Illich, it is not surprising that Gramsci's educational proposals showed a similar contrast.[11] The need to deal with scarcity and also the hostility of existing ruling elites (about which Illich offers little except 'hopeful trust') committed the radical educator, not only to specific, pre-ordained skills as part of the curriculum, but also to elements of compulsion in the whole educational process. Freedom needed to be much more a consequence of political and educational activity than a feature enshrined in the undertaking. Gramsci very much defended instruction against diffuse, social education, based on emotional intercourse. He upheld hierarchies of knowledge and intellectual elites, who had a responsibility to initiate others into the skills they would require to take over the running of society and make their own decisions about its future direction. He did not view paternalism as always and necessarily oppressive: the relationships between parent and child and teacher and pupil were appropriately asymmetrical. And he was strongly opposed to naturalistic development (spontaneity, learning by doing, suppression of authority), which he saw as abandoning students to the arbitrary influences of the environment, a more effective authoritarianism than introduction to the accumulated knowledge of humanistic, critical thought.

Given that Gramsci adhered to the notion of education as initiation into bodies of knowledge, there are two points to be made. First, the syllabus for such initiation should consist of the 'entire thought of the past' and, in particular, the most developed elements of thought in the ruling cultures of the past.

> If it is true that universal history is a chain made up of the efforts man has exerted to free himself from privilege, prejudice and idolatry, then it is hard to understand why the proletariat, which seeks to add another link to that chain, should not know how and why and by whom it was preceded, or what advantage it might derive from this knowledge.[12]

If the working class was to take over the administration of society, its members needed to respect the achievements of past ruling cultures and develop therefrom the capacity to construct their own executive strategies, in the widest possible sense. That would have to embrace both the technicalities involved in specific social functions (engineering, medicine, agriculture, theatre design, etc.) and an ethos of confidence and command, albeit adjusted to fit a system of democratic control. What had to be broken out of was confinement to defensive (i.e., subordinate) practices and a morality of resignation. The purpose of education in this respect was to put people into a position to exercise power and control and instil in them a credible desire to do so.

Second, the cardinal theme of the intiation process consisted of the transformation of spontaneous or popular philosophy into ordered, critical or scientific philosophy. The world-views, plans, beliefs, attitudes of the working class, as they ordinarily stood, were unsuited to social rule, not only because they accepted subordination as an underlying assumption, but also because they were formed and renewed in a disjointed, episodic fashion, which prevented their reaching the coherence required for organised execution. Scientific world-views, on the other hand, particularly since the rise of Renaissance science, accumulated and reviewed the thoughts of past ages and distant people, surveying and re-surveying the options, using standardised rules of evidence and rational argument to approach consistent sets of propositions capable of providing for successful social control. Knowledge based purely on personal experience and local debate lacked the breadth and rigour essential to planned social organisation. Gramsci also believed that workers and peasants were prone to intellectual laziness, preferring to cling to habitual superstitions and rules of thumb, rather than undertaking critical re-examinations of their beliefs and identifying the principles underlying the relevant practices. This simply betrayed an assumption that other people would always make the important social decisions. However, he though it very important that the transition from 'common sense' to 'good sense' or, further to genuine critical awareness, should be done sensitively. All philosophies, from the most humble to the most elevated, contained elements of superstition, folklore, experience and scientific reasoning; the hierarchic differences were not absolute, but only a matter of degree. Teachers attempting to supervise the development of popular thought to a more systematic outlook needed, therefore, to acquire their own 'science of folklore', to understand the existing beliefs and wisdoms of their students and to identify with the problems they faced. Superstition and folklore still had to be replaced by secular rationalism, rather than protected, but it had to be done carefully, respectfully, connecting science with existing wisdoms and addressing the underlying practicalities of working class and peasant life.

Finally, Gramsci held to the distinction between childhood and adult education. Children, he argued, should receive instruction in the classical liberal curriculum, with an emphasis upon collegiality and teachers who understood their responsibility to initiate the young into all the best of the existing culture. Schooling at that stage should be politically neutral, with religion and other ideologies kept out;

children should be encouraged to debate social and moral questions in a disinterested, methodical fashion. The main aim was to instil the cognitive repertoire necessary for critical and independent thought, including a considerable body of routine information and a mastery of the dominant culture (Gramsci opposed, for example, the teaching of regional dialects, seeing them as historically redundant).

In adulthood, education should remain informed by the sense of political purpose: to take over, to master the necessary operations of the world, to put everyone into a position where they were 'capable of thinking, studying and ruling - or controlling those who rule'.[13] That involved three areas of inquiry, narrower than the child's syllabus: (i) how to manage modern industrial society; (ii) how to understand the causes of the existing circumstances; and (iii) how to fight for the opportunity to put (i) into practice (i.e., how to struggle for political change). This adult education would be carried out primarily by the revolutionary political party. It was best conceived in that way because it needed to be informed by particular visions of the good society. Gramsci was doubtful about the validity of pluralism in this kind of education, inclining more towards singular ideological coherence. Once revolutionary changes were coming into view, with a thriving labour movement, two other institutions would take part: trade unions would give their members technical training, while factory councils would educate workers in political economy.

So here we have a stark opposition of view about the way forward in education, which can be summarised as follows: Illich is centrally concerned with the way the present education system fails and abuses the majority of the world's poor and lower class students and sees a parallel with similar failures on the part of all social institutions. His remedy is to 'de-institutionalise' the world, to break out of the preceding industrial and scientific trajectory and to establish a spontaneously associative and co-operative social order, hopefully undermining the ruling interests by non-co-operation from the bottom up. Gramsci was an enthusiast for what he saw as the progressive social developments witnessed in history, especially with the rise of science, political liberty and industry, originating in Europe. His solution to the domination of subordinate social classes was a political revolution that, not only unseated the bourgeoisie, but also installed a democratic working class fully capable of organising social activities to the satisfaction and elevation of everyone's needs. Where Illich wants education to become spontaneous, based on discontinuous inquiries and ad hoc gatherings, Gramsci wanted to extend the traditions of cumulative knowledge based on secular rationalism, by expanding established educational institutions to incorporate the whole population. Illich is the dissident Christian, happier in the backward economies of the Third World than in Europe, promoting libertarian anarchism of a distinctly moderate kind; Gramsci is the marxist, escaping the brutality and narrowness of peasant Sardinia, imprisoned by Mussolini, trying to realise the dreams of Hardy's Jude.[14]

Community Education and the C.A.R.E. Project

The reason for examining those polar opposites is to illuminate the implications of actual differences of approach in current practice. We may not wholly endorse the recommendations of either Illich or Gramsci, but we do have to decide how we see the future of necessary production and of social class. We can not, for instance, decide to get rid of class division, seek to uphold the modern industrial order and educate workers solely about welfare rights and group work. Both Illich and Gramsci are flawed, but they do set out a vocabulary that can help us to examine our initiatives.

The Community Education Forum linked weekends programme, discussed in the previous chapter, followed closely the approach proposed by Illich. The Forum, especially in the office of its Organiser, set itself up as a matching agency. Interested parties, from amongst community groups, could make a request for some kind of learning and be put in touch with others who shared their interests. The Forum itself did as little as possible to order such activities into any kind of curriculum, acting simply as a 'facilitator'. The weekends operated like a roving education fair, held in impromptu locations, each with different performers, free association, a playful atmosphere and a random ebb and flow of debate and distraction. The uniting factor was the continuity of the participants, although even that was limited. There was a premium upon sharing experience, getting to know others from similar circumstances, with perhaps similar problems or contrasting views or useful bits of advice. The body of organisers and tutors was very diverse, agreeing simply to contribute to an open-ended programme. Student choice was constantly extolled, on the understanding that that amounted to a democratic education and that it precluded the pursuit of an organised curriculum. Traditional schooling was derided as counter-productive and definite views on any aspects of community work were carefully discouraged by some of the main tutors, who pressed strongly for complete relativism in belief and 'non-direction' in practice. Much of the programme, indeed, was infused with an extreme ideology of 'non-directiveness' and of conservative libertarian (peace and reconciliation) politics, which tended to scoff at the disciplines of systematic inquiry.

C.A.R.E.'s work could be said to fall somewhere in between Illich and Gramsci. It contained elements of a network approach, where C.A.R.E. staff tried to put people with mutual interests in touch with each other and to break down bureaucratic barriers to information and knowledge. It differed from Gramsci insofar as it allowed a pluralism of view in adult teaching and showed more sympathy with existing working class culture. Yet it was much closer to Gramsci than was the Forum, inasmuch as it encouraged traditional academic skills like reading and writing, offered an ordered curriculum to the certificate class and gave much more open emphasis to a socialist purpose underlying all the initiatives.

Freire's Pedagogy

C.A.R.E. started with a strong interest in Freire's educational proposals: his notion of thematic investigation, his call for involvement in the social movements of the oppressed and his pedagogic model of dialogue and problem-posing, with teachers prepared to enter into debate with students on questions that they raised. His pedagogy was very influential in the work with the media in Northern Ireland. What became clear however during the three years (including a Freire seminar run at the Institute in 1979*) was that Freire's general conception is ambiguous in numerous respects. Bascially, Freire belongs to the existentialist tradition of Heidegger and Sartre, whose primary concern is with the will, with human desire and spirit. He is best seen as addressing himself to problems of the will, to the oppression of desire in his students. His pedagogic method is designed to get people to re-orient themselves in relation to the world that surrounds them. Instead of existing in a state of acceptance, of submission, of fatalism (which he calls the 'culture of silence'), the educator should lead them to think of themselves as creators, as actors upon the world, shaping it, changing it according to their wishes. As he argues, that involves a profound alteration of outlook, a dramatically different conception of being-in- or being-with-the world; instead of submission to another's will (heteronomy), object-ification of one's own will, control of one's own surroundings (autonomy). Unless this is confined to the most individualistic interpretation, which Freire explicitly refutes, it implies precisely the cultural re-orientation that Illich wishes to reverse.

However, Freire stops too soon and is plagued by the unclarity which so often creeps into quasi-Hegelian thought; he relapses into the maze of 'authenticity'. He complains that regular schooling demoralises the lower class students and thereby creates the very heteronomy education is supposed to destroy. And he argues that many so-called revolutionary political parties disguise a dictatorial leadership, which creates a similar dependence amongst their ordinary membership and supporters. He calls instead for authentic liberating praxis, based on dialogical co-operation, the freedom of the oppressed 'to speak their own word' and a refusal of all institutional hierarchies or rigidities. Part of this can be reconciled with democratic socialist advance; another part is too abstract to amount to much more than rhetorical posturing (betraying his religious past). The rest is close to Illich in proposing a communitarian undermining of oppressive institutions from below.

So Freire can be seen to lead both ways: towards Gramsci (and Marx and G.B. Shaw) in calling for an injection of Promethean fire into the self-image of the oppressed; and towards Illich (and early Sartre and various anarchists) in seeking a structureless, 'de-institutionalised' popular upheaval. That vagueness derives from the existentialism to which he owes so much. The notion of authenticity is notoriously fluid, adaptable to any and every conception of original 'human nature' or 'complete social freedom'. It is an abstract rhetorical device that leads to circular argument and avoids any specific empirical

---

*   For which many thanks are due to Sean Courtney.

definition. It becomes what Barrow calls a 'likely story', virtually impossible to refute and encouraging its defenders to meet all criticism with some argument about dissent proving the critic's vulnerability to a distorting, hostile world.[15]

Freire's central ambiguity is apparent when he is most specific: at a developed stage in the process of problem-posing education, after thematic investigation, the coding of themes into telling images, decoding in discussion circles, etc.,[16] he recommends that experts be brought in to stimulate discussion on specialist concerns. At no point does he make any attempt to specify what counts as an expert. One can only assume that he accepts the conventional qualifications for such status and allows that traditional schooling of specialists will continue side-by-side with his dialogical work amongst the poor and exploited. Nevertheless, he says nothing about which schools of thought to adopt in, say, economics, nor even how to make one's own evaluation of the incompatible schools. Whatever his disclaimers about commitment to radical change and liberation of the oppressed, he falls into the category of 'child-centred educators who emphasise principles of procedure with a seemingly cavalier disregard for matters of direction and content'.[17] His attempts to rescue this position, by suggesting that authentic libertarian education will necessarily seek out correct or adequate understandings, is simply tautological. (Milton Friedman is the authentic liberator in economics for many Friedmanites, including a surprising number of anarchists and anti-statists).

What must be faced, and what Freire and Illich both try to evade, is the need to specify definite bodies of knowledge and principles of inquiry, which fit in with the political aspirations of the educational project. Freire's dichotomy of problem-posing versus banking is simply unsound, unless problem-posing is reduced to a matter of engaging students' interest. When he goes on to call for a virtual elimination of the distinction between teachers and taught, he goes altogether too far. No doubt learning can profitably arise from completely symmetrical cultural circles. The question is, what kind of learning do we want or need to promote? (and how can trained educators, skilled technicians and other intellectuals best contribute to that process?) And that brings us back to the need for practical definitions of human liberation in a very imperfect world. The intellectual disabling that Freire identifies in 'banking' is far from universal and is not the result of teaching, as such, nor even of rigidly prescribed instruction. Many critical, inventive and far-seeing human beings have emerged from the most rigorous instructional institutions, however much they may look back upon it with hatred; rigour, systematic condescension and brutality should not be conflated, as they often are in the aftermath of disgust. Indeed, it is hard to see how genuinely critical intellects, capable of participating in democratic social management and organisation, can develop other than through the stimulation of vigorous, ordered and sustained schooling. If that is not to be for the oppressed, then either we accept the reactionary claim that they are incapable of responding to such searching demands or else we declare that that kind of critical development will not be needed in some 'post-industrial' society of the future. It may otherwise be held that community educators are working with people, including activists, who, by virtue of the scale of the desired changes, will necessarily be marginal to the whole enterprise and that educational vigour is consequently misplaced. What needs to be distinguished here is marginal status within a larger social project that offers real hope of eradicating class subordination in the long run and a general social project which casts community activists in a marginal social position throughout; that is, the difference between tactical and permanent marginality. Tactical marginality necessitates education with a view to future control; permanent marginality should be left to conservatives who appreciate the subtle virtues of hereditary power.

None of this implies that problem-posing or open debate without teacher privilege are undesirable. The point to be made is twofold: first, pedagogic method is secondary to the overall purpose of the education; second, education aiming to promote the eradication of class division must include, at the very least, some old-fashioned instruction, set into an ordered curriculum, which includes basic information and skills required to execute necessary management tasks.

Where it is useful, the problem-posing attitude on the part of teachers does not mean getting students to define all the questions and conferring validity upon all the proffered answers. It is neither an epistemological relativism nor an abdication of the responsibility to teach. What it is is a meeting of the ways between the practicalities of working class life and the contribution of disciplined inquiry. Ordering a curriculum with regard to the concerns of students active in a social movement like community action enables educators to construct a programme that engages their attention and is capable of promoting more effective resolutions of the problems. But, even if student centred approaches are used, the educator still needs to interpose a body of knowledge and sensibility that will contribute to real democracy, hopefully in an atmosphere of mutual consent, but ultimately irrespective of the students' wishes.

Teachers must avoid the kind of autocracy which undermines any democratic sensibility; but they must, nevertheless, teach[18] and include in their teaching much of the best of what has been handed down by centuries of intellectual contest and co-operation. Working class movements can not liberate humanity *ex nihilo*; they only stand a chance if they use the equipment painstakingly created and passed on to them by their precursors. Not all authority is oppressive; authority based on reason is a valuable inheritance for all democrats.

NOTES

1. Weber was the least happy of the three about it, suffering enormous anxiety about the transformation of the world into a field of mere functions, deprived of meaning. But even he, perhaps he above all, demanded of all reformers and progressives a 'matter-of-factness' that would allow them reluctantly to accept the disenchantment of the

world and do battle on behalf of its desirable possibilities. To do otherwise, he thought, was to turn one's back on human affairs altogether.

2. M.F.D. Young (ed.), *Knowledge and Control* (Collier-Macmillan, London, 1971); M.F.D. Young and G. Whitty (eds.), *Society, State and Schooling* (Falmer Press, Ringmer, 1977); G. Bernbaum, *Knowledge and Ideology in the Sociology of Education* (Macmillan, London, 1977); R. Dale et al (eds.), *Schooling and Capitalism* (Routledge and Kegan Paul/O.U.P., London, 1976).

3. Ivan Illich, *De-schooling Society* (Penguin, Harmondsworth, 1973) p. 20.

4. Ibid., p. 110 "A world of ever-rising demands is not just evil - it can be spoken of only as Hell".

5. Ibid., pp. 28-9.

6. Ibid., pp. 106, 108 and 114-5. Most of this passage refers to the final chapter of Illich's book, entitled "Rebirth of Epimethean Man'.

7. Ibid., pp. 66-7.

8. Ibid., p. 45.

9. Ibid., p. 27.

10. Mannacorda put it thus: that, for Gramsci, "it is not the existence of discipline which compromises liberty, but the type of power which ordains it". Quoted in Entwistle, *Antonio Gramsci: Conservative Schooling for Radical Politics* (Routledge and Kegan Paul, London, 1977) p. 139.

11. Although Gramsci was writing during and after the First World War, too much can be made of this; there can be no doubt that the presuppositions of his educational theory would have showed a similar contrast to Illich's even had he lived after 1945. However, it must be borne in mind that his writings were fragmentary and specific theories on issues like education necessarily involve selection and surmise. See Entwistle op. cit. and the review of that book in *Social History* Vol. 6 No. 2, May 1981 pp. 209-227 (esp. 221-223) Keith Neild and John Seed 'Waiting for Gramsci'.

12. *Political Writings 1910-20* (Q. Hoare (ed.) (trans. J. Mathews) International Publishers, New York, 1977) p. 13.

13. *Selections from the Prison Notebooks of Antonio Gramsci* (Q. Hoare and Nowell Smith (eds. and trans.) Lawrence and Wishart, London, 1971) p. 40.

14. " 'Why should you care so much for Christminster?' she said positively. 'Christminster cares nothing for you, poor dear!' 'Well, I do and I can't help it. I love the place although I know how it hates all men like me - the so-called self-taught - how it scorns our laboured acquisitions, when it should be the first to respect them; how it sneers at our false quantities and mispronounciations, when it should say, I see you want help, my poor friend! ...... Nevertheless, it is the centre of the universe to me, because of my early dream; and nothing can alter it. Perhaps it will soon wake up, and be generous. I pray so!' ...." Thomas Hardy *Jude the Obscure* (Penguin, Harmondsworth, 1978) p. 391.

15. Robin Barrow, *Radical Education: A Critique of Free-schooling and De-schooling* (Martin Robertson, London, 1978) p. 4 passim. See also the classic critical marxist account of existentialism, T.W. Adorno, *The Jargon of Authenticity* (trans. Knut Tarowski and Frederic Will) (Routledge and Kegan Paul, London, 1973).

16. Paolo Freire, *Pedagogy of the Oppressed* (trans. M.B. Ramos) (Penguin, Harmondsworth, 1972) esp. Chapter 3.

17. R.S. Peters (ed.), *The Philosophy of Education* (O.U.P., Oxford, 1973) Peters' own 'Aims of Education - A Conceptual Inquiry' (pp. 11-29) p. 27.

18. Jane L. Thompson (ed.), *Adult Education for a Change* (Hutchinson, London, 1980), foreword by Keith Jackson (pp. 9-18) pp. 17-18: "Progressive educational attitudes about equality can easily lead to irresponsibility on the part of those who are paid and expected to extend students, not merely to reassure them".

Chapter 11

COMMUNITY EDUCATION AND SOCIAL MOVEMENTS

The whole discussion about adult education and social change, about the role of adult education in community action, about its relationship to the working class, discussed in the preceding chapters in this book revolves around four categories, choice, authority, relevance and purpose. Community education, because of its initial concern with the question of how to reach the working class and how to relate to many of the problems and issues they face stimulated a great deal of debate about choice and authority, which might be said to be the fulcrum of democratic education. But ultimately they are intelligible only in relation to the question of purpose, with relevance as a kind of red herring.

In relation to choice, as is repeatedly pointed out, adult students are not compelled to attend education programmes. In most instances they are there out of choice. That point is worth remembering since it is one of the factors making adult learning different from childhood learning and giving rise to discussion of teaching methods specifically designed for adults (androgogy, rather than pedagogy). Without some kind of consent and, in many cases, considerable curiosity, even the most impeccable programme or course will have no students. It is precisely that simple truth that has attracted many socialists to the work of people like Freire, in an attempt to break out of the cliques and ghettoes of much marxist political education. Yet even that element of choice is far from absolute. Many students are driven to seek career advancement; others inhabit specific associations, fields of practice, etc., which encourage attendance at conferences and courses; some are actually obliged to fulfil educational requirements once they have decided to pursue a certain occupational path or, on lamentably rare occasions, because they have joined a political organisation. On top of that, it is clear that financial provision for adult education can be a major influence upon student choice: how many managers, teachers, local authority officers attend mid-week, in-service courses, all expenses paid, out of an untrammelled passion for the subject? (How many fewer attend at weekends?) If the kind of day-release benefits that surround the management and professional conference circuit were universally available, choice would not remain indifferent. Conversely, even the need to attract students is not absolute and it is qualified further if we relinquish the demand for large numbers (we should not assume that every course should appeal to the greatest number of people, like television pap dished up for the advertisers).

But the most important aspect of choice concerns the relationship between democracy and the marketplace. How is democratic control related to consumer sovereignty? Who is to control the 'production' of education? What will be the relationship between teachers and students?

It is easy to claim that democracy amounts to student control over an education programme, with teaching staff conforming to students' wishes. But that ignores the role of objective aspirations. Bourdieu's work is interesting here:

> In general, children and their families make their own choices by reference to the constraints which determine them. Even when the choices seem to follow simply from taste or vocational sense, they nevertheless indicate the roundabout effects of objective conditions. In other words, the structure of the objective chances of social mobility and, more precisely, of the chances of social mobility by means of education, conditions attitudes to school (and it is precisely these attitudes which are most important in defining the chances of access to education, of accepting the values or norms of the school and of succeeding within the framework and thus rising in society) through subjective hopes (shared by all individuals defined by the same objective future, and reinforced by the group's pressure for conformity), which are no more than objective chances intuitively perceived and gradually internalised.[1]

What people choose is influenced by what their circumstances encourage them to want. If an objective is really incredible, we are unlikely to set out to achieve it. If some pursuits are familiar and safe, we may be inclined to stick with them, rather than risk the unknown. If previous education has arbitrarily humiliated us when we attempted certain tasks, we may be reluctant to try them again. If whole areas of knowledge and the kinds of excitement, terror, headaches and boredom they arouse are unknown to us, we may lack even the vocabulary to inquire about them.

Working class culture often discourages people from having a high opinion of their intellect. Community action circles often encourage people to interest themselves in some subject, but not others, in, say, housing, but not industry or in group dynamics, but not politics. The inclinations that community education students bring with them are conditioned by such influences.

If democratic education is to have any sense, students must be consulted about the programmes they enter, both in terms of curriculum and standard procedures and in relation to particular incidents and grievances. Teachers have a responsibility to open up courses to that kind of discussion. They also have a responsibility to promote what generations of democrats and scholars and others have bequeathed them: namely, bodies of knowledge and principles of practice, of varying quality and definition. Teachers need to contribute to the debate, not only their own specialism, but also an understanding of the way, in most fields, education is more than a series of discrete events; that it often achieves more when it takes the form of an ordered curriculum, especially at an introductory level; that students in most subjects do not always learn best by starting wherever seems best to them and playing it by ear. (They should also bear in mind that the students who will tend to benefit most from such structureless approaches will be those who get most advantages from the world outside the classroom, a result which is hard to reconcile with democratic objectives.)

Democracy is not the same as consumer demand. Popular (student) consultation is a necessary, but not a sufficient condition. Democracy also involves upholding the best of the past in terms of human enlightenment and organising affairs with a view to achieving democratic control over the whole of society. Democratic, and especially socialist, educators have to argue for programmes that contribute to such a future and for choices based on such high aspirations. They are not there simply 'to reassure people' that whatever they want is okay. They are there to fight for democracy, as well as respond to democratic pressures. There will always be an element of contradiction in that, requiring political judgment to resolve.

Authority
There is a huge difference between people who claim to reject all authority, as a universally oppressive force, inimical to human freedom and others who distinguish rational from irrational authority and oppose only the second. The first of those positions is a luxurious piece of nonsense, a vacuous abstraction, which can only be maintained by people distant from the responsibilities of power. It is comparable to the response to political imperfection which declares all politics corrupt and unacceptable, a throwing up of the hands in smug resignation. All social organisation must be based on acceptance of definite decisions, respect for determinate judgments and codes of practice, even though, in time, most prove to be no more than provisional. To reject all authority is at once a delusion and a demand for a kind of total freedom that can only lead ultimately to the law of the jungle, which would hardly benefit the oppressed. The real question, for anyone concerned with practical political progress, is about the derivation of authority. To what do we grant provisional jurisdiction? and how do we come by such judgments?

The anarchistic position rests upon a strong form of naturalism: people will be most free when they are most unregulated by structured social order; liberty is compromised by social organisation and command; human beings are innately convivial and creative and would express such positive traits more fully if only the institutionalised weight of the past were shaken off their backs, if only they were left alone. The problem with that kind of argument is that it is not only finally unverifiable (every instance of its being contradicted can be dismissed as evidence that we still are not free) and extremely implausible, but also quite meaningless.

Educational practice which starts from that kind of absolute relativism has strictly limited potential. It can usefully draw students out into public declaration and discussion of their own concerns and such sharing of experience has an important part to play in any education. Students undoubtedly consolidate learning by putting themselves on the line in public and by making connections between what is being learned and what is already of interest. But we still have the question, a sharing of experience to what end? (let alone the problem of a conceptual vocabulary for any such expression). If we say that educators should let students determine their own purposes without interference, then we relinquish responsibility for the sensibilities aroused to the external environment. Unless that environment is conducive to the aims of the educational exercise, the students are not being helped.

If we start from a desire to promote a social movement, to use education to promote and give shape to a particular cause, then clearly we must grant authority to principles which fit the cause. That is where Gramsci is interesting. The cause for him was popular social rule, extending the benefits of existing society, combatting the flaws and satisfying the needs of the great majority of the population. The syllabus for education in that field should comprise the best knowledge of the past, giving definite authority to the traditions of rational, secular and scientific practice. But the curriculum had to possess another element: it had to be based upon a new authority, the intellectual autonomy of the working class. What was wrong with existing education was not its syllabus, nor even its discipline and hierarchies; it was that it extolled the culture of bourgeois privilege. Indispensable knowledge was distorted by association with bourgeois authority and sensibility ('The existing school system was directed at making the views of the bourgeoisie universal, in particular the feeling of nationalism'). For Gramsci, a liberating education for the working class had to possess considerable autonomy, to be run by the movement, so that a different sensibility could be instilled. The classical traditions, skills, disciplines had to be taught but they had to develop into an independent culture, at once capable of re-organising the whole of civilisation (so that the working class must not be defined narrowly in terms of, say, the poor or manual workers) and distinctively attuned to the interests of the working class.

Every class that achieved power, he argued, prepared itself first by developing its own education. An independent tradition was established, in everything from books and newspapers to actual classes, which organised the skills and self-esteem necessary to run an entirely different kind of state. This was not a matter of glorifying the existing culture of the aspiring class, but of assimilating and extending the most liberating potential in all fields of knowledge and supplying a new corps of intellectuals proficient in the widest possible range of necessary and life-enhancing skills. To do that, however, entailed a recognition of the underestimated contribution already made by the class even while it had remained subordinate. An appreciation of the unrecognised abilities amongst working class people and the far from passive role they had played in the development of bourgeois civilisation would give a great impetus to the revaluation of the class self-image. So it was not a matter of counterposing middle class culture against working class culture, but of organising a working class culture that removed the barriers and distortions that social privilege had put in the way of knowledge. Cultural self-respect was a starting point, from which independent education had to expand in all directions, until the new culture was more truly universal than the existing dominant one. In so doing the authority of rational inquiry and humanistic practice would be both enhanced and democratised. Authority and tradition would not disappear; they would become more firmly rational and universal. There would be one truth for everybody, regardless of class, sex, race or nation. Freedom of knowledge and inquiry would be based upon social and intellectual foundations that offered a real chance of being fulfilled.

Relevance
It is a common complaint that much of compulsory schooling is irrelevant to working class kids, that the realities of life-after-school are ignored in the setting of the curriculum. If education is to appeal to working class people, it must possess more relevance to the lives they actually live. Within this school of thought, there is pressure, for example, for less academically successful working class children to be prepared for unemployment, instead of being fed on illusions about a career.

Any argument about relevance must include some notion of relevance to what? To answer that we need to know what the purpose of the education is supposed to be. If we are not careful about this, there is a real danger of ghettoism in tailoring programmes to the needs of people whose prospects are doomed to remain extremely restricted. Is the point to ease the burden of belonging to a subordinate social class, to make subordination more bearable? Or is it to get rid of unnecessary subordination and to remove the restrictions upon working class students' potential? If we are talking of educational support for social action, then that decision is especially pertinent.

It is worth distinguishing two separate aspects of the question of relevance: first, the problem of ensuring that students find the educational programme interesting, that they are attracted on to it in the first place and that their enthusiasm is sustained; second, the content of the programme, what kinds and combinations of subjects are actually appropriate to the furtherance of a social movement. These have been called the experiential and cognitive aspects of the question. Relevance, insofar as it is regarded as desirable, need not necessarily be established through the cognitive character of the programme. The sense of irrelevance felt by those who do poorly at school is less a result of school subjects being valueless than of the experience of being at school and of moving on afterwards making such subjects valueless *for them*. It is quite plausible to imagine the same students finding the same subjects valuable (perhaps only in the long run in some areas), were they to attend a school and take part in a community that filled them with pride and dignity, instead of failing them. A very similar case can be made for saying that the general alienation of the working class population from the theatre is less to do with the repertoires of the drama companies than a result of the whole experience of attending a ritual beset with middle class symbolism. To call for a wholly revised repertoire is to miss a major part of the point.

In education, short of a dramatic collapse in modern industrial production, it is clear that the curriculum of compulsory schooling, with continual marginal adjustments, will remain highly relevant to the school 'successes', to managers, engineers, skilled technicians, entrepreneurs and apprentices of all kinds. Much of the basic training and many of the more abstract disciplines seem reasonably suited to the demands of contemporary society. Are we then to say that a wholly different curriculum is appropriate for people who do not make the official grade? and, if so, why?

Education that aims to promote a social movement, like community action, has to adjust any notion of relevance to the aspirations of the movement; it has to be relevant to the kind of society the movement is trying to achieve and to the campaigns along the way, rather than to the existing social circumstances. It has to attract and hold students who have those aspirations and it has to provide cognitive stimulation which will enhance their efforts.

As far as experiential features are concerned, the main need is for a programme that is committed to the general cause adopted by the students. Both the atmosphere of the educational events as a whole and the behaviour of individual educators must show respect for and genuine interest in what the movement is up to. Students must feel that their concerns will be shared by everyone and taken seriously. They must also be encouraged to believe that credible goals are achievable, although it will be part of the education to separate justifiable optimism from wishful thinking (what Manning once called 'the optimism of the uninformed').

Part of taking students seriously will involve giving attention to their particular concerns. The experiences they have had, the obstacles that confront them and the shifting objectives they have in view are amongst their defining characteristics. To respect the students must imply deliberately allowing time to explore those elements of their lives, either in class or informally. All effective education, especially of adults, with years of experience behind them, is going to involve, at some stage, a drawing of connections between the subjects being learned and the rest of the life being lived. There is, to our knowledge, nothing to indicate that such connections are most successfully made if the educator keeps them off the syllabus. On the contrary, discussion of such experiences and concerns can play an important part in attracting students on to the course and enriching their understanding of what is to be taught (to say nothing of giving teachers a better grasp of issues outside their experience).

It is not necessary, however, to limit the rest of the cognitive side of the programme to students' immediate concerns. Plenty of subject areas can be explored without prior student approval, provided the students' interest and trust in the teachers are sustained. Many such unrequested activities may ultimately prove the most fruitful and stimulating pursuits. It is not possible to assess the 'relevance' of a subject before we know a certain amount about it. A social movement like community action can not afford to proscribe subject areas which will become relevant as and when political progess is made. The only way a democratic education can deal with this is to encourage teachers to examine the movement's aspirations objectively and seek to persuade students to engage in disciplines which are likely to be needed in the long run.

Overall, 'relevance' is too blunt a category to be much use in shaping such education programmes. While it has some place in ensuring that students experience a sense of stimulation and respect, it should be applied sparingly in discussion of the cognitive content of a course. While the course as a whole must address itself to objectives that are appropriate to the movement, the value of some disciplines may be sufficiently distant as to seem irrelevant at the outset.

Purpose

The long-term criteria for a curriculum can only be set in relation to a general purpose. What is to count as progress and as development? What will be the future of industrial society and of social class? Many of the means of achieving objectives in those areas necessarily remain uncertain and it will be a vital part of a programme to discuss the options. But some ends are clearly incompatible and it is not clear how a programme constructed by people who flatly disagree about such aims can work out well.

Social movements, as opposed to political parties, rarely have unitary objectives. They comprise widely disparate aims, united for tactical reasons. The early British labour movement, for example, contained the disagreement between radical populists, like Cobbett, and the precursors of socialism, like the Chartists.[2] That dispute, about what was to count as 'really useful knowledge', set Cobbett's version of de-schooling, emphasizing practical skills, learning within the home and hostility towards schoolteachers, against the Chartist notion of spearhead knowledge, with its emphasis on literacy, politics and anti-clerical conceptions of science. Cobbett's naturalism involved a personalisation of politics and a nostalgia for the interests of small producers; it was based upon hostility to the new industrial order as such, including the rationalism that accompanied it: 'Cobbett, in fact, helped to create and nourish the anti-intellectualism, and the theoretical opportunism (masked as 'practical' empiricism) which remained an important characteristic of the British labour movement.' 'Just as he developed, not a critique of a political *system*, nor even of 'legitimacy', but an invective against 'Old Corruption', so he reduced economic analysis to a polemic against the *parasitism* of certain vested interests.'[3] Mainstream Chartism sought to encourage, not the practical skills of the self-sufficient small farmer and healthy living, but the development of an indigenous working class leadership within a movement that would confront the new industrial order and reform it. This involved a broad conception of the practical, not counterposed to 'liberal' education: 'Despite the stress on a relation to the knower's experience, there is no narrowly *pragmatic* conception of knowledge here. Knowledge is not just a political instrument; the search for 'truth' matters.'[4] Within this broad sweep, incorporating 'a rich literary culture' and 'a widespread interest in the natural sciences', there were key areas of immediate importance to the movement. This 'spearhead knowledge' consisted of (a) political analysis, (b) social science and (c) the causes of poverty and exploitation. Although this tradition, like Cobbett, was deeply critical of provided schooling, unlike him they revered the acquisition of academic knowledge and knowledge of all kinds and they shared Paine's hostility to both monarchy and priesthood ('Paine taught radicals that monarchy, being based on so irrational a device as inheritance, tended to 'buy reason up' and that priests were employed to keep people ignorant.')[5]

Community action, as all radical social movements of today, is composed of similarly incongruous elements. The battle over production continues, 150 years on, as does the 'running debate within radicalism between those who argued that we remain ignorant and need to get knowledge and those who inverted the intellectual pyramid and argued that 'we' were really wiser than 'they'.'[6] That is still the debate between science and practical experience, sophistication and simplicity, as unresolved in educational circles as it was when the industrial order first began to devastate the stabilities of rural life.

Education involves a commitment to some notion of what it is to be educated, not in a universal sense, but in relation to some implied or explicit social objectives. It can not prosper under conditions where the educator has lost all sense of where we should be going. Indeed, that sort of despondency, even nihilism, within the teaching profession seriously undermines children's hopes and application. Education that is mounted by teachers and administrators who throw up their hands and declare that the future is wholly uncertain, that any scenario is as valid as any other, remove one essential impetus for learning. Learning can and does happen all the time, casually and without supervision, and it is important to combat the effective condescension of our society towards manual and uncategorized intelligence. Kirkwood is right to insist, in a recent *Adult Education* debate, that 'matters of immediate interest and concern' to working class students can be successfully married to general questions and wider understandings of the context in which particularities arise. He is right to reject 'a belief common among many that working people don't or can't think, and that practical work processes are divorced from thought'.[7] There is no unfathomable gulf between practical knowledge or 'know-how' and a grasp of underlying principles which enable us rationally to manipulate our practices and surroundings in pursuit of planned objectives.[8] But neither is there any immediate or necessary association of the two. Education has a large and indispensable role to play in precisely that mediation.

We do not inhabit a world in which spontaneous fellow-feeling can resolve our social problems. In a world of massive economic scarcity and brutal conflicts of interest, the politics of goodwill amount to a straightforward deception: their adherents are not confronting our problems in a new and more wholesome way; they are running away from them and taking their followers with them, leaving in the driving seat others, already in power, who have no intention whatsoever of wandering off in search of gentler pastures. Goodwill politics underestimate capitalism in at least two respects: they misjudge the determination of ruling interests to hold on to privilege at almost any cost and they do capitalist economic enterprise the injustice of overlooking its gigantic contribution to the satisfaction of basic human needs, the enlargement of horizons and the securing of partial political liberties (in the words of Robinson: '. . . . the misery of being exploited by capitalists is nothing compared to the misery of not being exploited at all'[9]). Progressive politics have to deal with both those things: they have to defeat political intransigence and they have to improve upon, not abandon, the massive energies capitalist economies have produced. Anything that fails to fulfil those strictures is a reverse, not an advance. Vilifying capitalism for being mean or greedy or inflexible is either insufficient or downright wrong.

Democratic or progressive politics have the purpose of gaining more control over all social affairs for the mass of the population. Control is not the same thing as consultation, where no more than a chance to voice grievances is conceded by power-holders. But, if control is a higher demand, it also requires the knowledge and ability to run social institutions better, rather than just kicking out the incumbents to satisfy some kind of moral indignation. Of course, most democrats, and certainly socialists, demand great changes in those institutions that we want democratised; but there are definite limits to such transformation, which anti-capitalist rhetoric often brushes aside. The most important limit is quite simply that there is no possibility of progressive democratisation except on the basis of the kind of industrial order that capitalism has generated. It is that sophisticated system of production that has to be run rationally, imaginatively and in a democratic manner. Such administration requires skills which do not arise spontaneously from working class experience. Nor are they derivable from initiation into face-to-face integrity, inner peace and contentment. They can only proceed from instruction in a substantial body of information, skills and principles, and in the encouragement of a Promethean instinct. Gramsci, in other words, had a firmer grasp of the necessary purpose that does Illich and it is interesting to see that Freire's own progress has increasingly distanced him from Illich's naturalism (see his work on Guinea-Bissau).

Yet such discussions can not remain as generalised as that. Gramsci, admittedly writing in the first quarter of this century, committed the error of triumphialism at times; he adopted the same heroic account of 'man's conquest of nature' unravelling through historical time that capitalism's own ideologists propound. That is, as Williams has argued, an oversimplification characteristic of the marxist tradition. If Illich and writers like him allow a lament about the disenchantment of the world to blind them to real achievements and necessities, Gramsci and some other marxists fail to acknowledge at all the implications of disenchantment. The real task is to elaborate a progressive unfolding of the enlightenment, which protects secular rationalism from religious and naturalist reaction, but admits a more subtle understanding of the relationship between human will and natural or physical surroundings. The Promethean drive for human control needs to be upheld, but we need to qualify its overweening heroism. Education for progressive social action needs to take its inspiration accordingly.

NOTES

1.   Pierre Bourdieu 'The school as a conservative force' in Dale et al (eds.) *Schooling and Capitalism* (Routledge and Kegan Paul and Open University Press, London, 1976) pp. 110-117, p. 111.   Also: ". . . the influence of peer groups . . . . reinforces, among the least privileged children, the influence of the family milieu and the general social environment, which tend to discourage ambitions seen as excessive and always somewhat suspect in that they imply rejection of the individual's social origins. Thus, everything conspires to bring back those who, as we say, 'have no future' to 'reasonable' hopes (or 'realistic' ones, as Lewin calls them) and in fact, in many cases, to make them give up hope'. p. 112.

2.   See Richard Johnson, 'Really useful knowledge': radical education and working class culture, 1790-1848' in J. Clarke et al. (eds.) *Working Class Culture* (Hutchinson, London, 1979) pp. 79-102.

3.   E.P. Thompson, *The Making of the English Working Class* (Penguin, Harmondsworth, 1968) p. 830 and p. 832.

4.   Johnson, op. cit., p. 86.

5.   Ibid., p. 78.

6.   Ibid., p. 85.

7.   Colin Kirkwood, 'Adult Education and the Concept of Community' in *Adult Education* Vol. 51 No. 3 (1978) p. 147.

8.   R.S. Peters (ed.) *The Concept of Education* (Routledge and Kegan Paul, London, 1967), Ch. 1 (esp. pp. 6-9).

9.   Joan Robinson, *Economic Philosophy* (Penguin, Harmondsworth, 1964) p. 46.

CONCLUSION

By the beginning of the 1980's, despite the growth and activity of community groups during the previous decade, neither the 'national' question nor the enormous social and economic problems facing the working class in Northern Ireland, are any nearer solution. In many respects the situation has worsened. Industrial decline continues at an alarming rate creating a situation where it is realistic to talk about the de-industrialisation of the Province. Unemployment and poverty have become the lot of an ever increasing section of the population, making Northern Ireland one of the poorest and most deprived regions in western Europe.

Yet despite this common deprivation the gap between the two communities has grown in the wake of continuing violence. The 'bridge' built in the seventies by community action increasingly appears flimsy and weak in relation to the larger political and religious divisions between the two communities. At a local level the achievements of community groups in attempting to gain access to, or control over, services and resources are minimal. The bureaucratic structures remain largely unaltered by their efforts. This failure, plus the growth in poverty and unemployment throughout the Province illustrates the inability of community groups to improve the lot of the working class in the Province, except in marginal areas e.g. the provision of social and recreational facilities.

The experience of community action in Northern Ireland over the last decade has underlined its relative failure to have any real influence on those larger social, economic and political forces influencing and shaping events in the Province. What started as an apparently radical social movement, loosely uniting elements in the Protestant and Catholic working class, has increasingly become an extension of the welfare state, encouraging self-help or acting as outreach agents for statutory housing, welfare or educational authorities and organisations in the Province.

There are a number of reasons for this development, some peculiar to Northern Ireland, some common the community groups everywhere, e.g. political divisions between Catholics and Protestants over the national question which can still, on occasions, override any sense of common grievance; different views about the nature and role of community action; a tendency for community activities and community activists to be co-opted by the state. Community work in Northern Ireland is increasingly financed through, and thus to some extent controlled by, government departments and local authorities. The latter are closely involved in assisting community groups to run local resource centres and in the provision of educational support for community activists.

This development has had the effect, as in Great Britain, of formalising the structure of community groups, emphasising the need for formal constitutions and procedures thus directing popular initiatives through safe and well tested channels which meet the needs of local bureaucracies rather than those of community groups. Thus many community groups in Northern Ireland, despite having gone through stages leading up to successful conflict strategies in the early years of community action in the Province and successfully managing their own communities in periods of crisis, are increasingly drawn into the state welfare system to become professional or semi-professional community workers.

The experience of community groups in Northern Ireland is a striking example of the British genius for taking the radical edge off community action by creating various forms of co-optive machinery. The experience amongst the black population in England is somewhat similar. One American commentator on the racial problem in England remarked: 'This country's positive genius for co-opting fledgling black leadership, smothering it with kindness, may be one of the reasons why there is so little likelihood of a major, politically significant civil rights movement developing here.'

The work of the C.A.R.E. project discussed in this book attempted to counter that trend, to help build a social movement rather than support a semi-professional activity. However its successes were limited and its influence slight, given the resources at its disposal, the strength of the forces operating in the opposite direction, and its institutional base.

The latter provided a degree of flexibility and freedom to experiment which is often denied to adult educators working in other institutional settings. It was possible to prise open some of the resources of the university and place them at the disposal of working class communities. However, this was not without its problems and difficulties. The practical implication of putting university resources at the disposal of the community often meant utilising those resources to support all sorts of community activities and using university premises for meetings and discussions about the wide range of social, economic and political problems facing the working class in those communities. This, in principle, is nothing new for university adult education departments. It is very much part of the development role of most adult tutors i.e. making contact with groups in the general community and assisting them in their work. However there is less conflict with the university establishment when this work takes the form of assisting a local preservation society, rather than helping a group of residents fight the local council! Universities have their own political views which influence their position in such matters.

In the activities discussed in this book there were inevitable tensions as a result of that situation which were only eased because the work was regarded as 'experimental' or 'research'. In the long run a university base for such activities has inherent limitations; the marginality of this sort of work to the institution as a whole; the continuing battle to prove that it is educational, not political. However the major limitation is the lack of any radical sense of social *purpose* as distinct from a broad sense of social *responsibility*.

Of course committed educators can, and do, create their own space in such circumstances. There is no denying that much good work is undertaken by various institutions as a result of such institutional 'guerrillas' carrying out sorties to capture resources and expertise for working class community action. However if the Promethean drive discussed in the last chapter is to be successful then it will require a more open, frank commitment to radical social change than is possible in such circumstances. It will require a sense of social and political purpose; a view of the world as it is and as it could be; a dream of the future and an ability to link this to the educational process. It must in fact offer an alternative vision.

Until recently, adult education initiatives concerned with the alternative vision have been seriously neglected in the discussion about the role of adult education in community action. Yet the evidence is that historically such alternatives played an important role in encouraging, supporting and strengthening movements for social change. As indicated in this book many initiatives in community education are not really radical educational alternatives in that tradition, offering an alternative sense of social purpose, but merely extensions of the prevailing liberal ideology in adult education.

The question posed by the Council for Continuing Education in Northern Ireland - 'What is the social purpose of the education service given the reality we confront and the future we expect?' - must be answered in terms which affirm the right of men and women, here and elsewhere, to challenge that reality and shape their future. That process will be greatly assisted by the establishment of new, radical, educational institutions and networks concerned to offer a different set of aims and objectives, prepared to challenge the ways things are, to break the cultural hegemony inherent in existing educational provision, to offer a vision of a new society based on equality, fraternity and concern for social justice.

Here in Northern Ireland there is an urgent need to create such an alternative adult education system or institution, committed to the twin processes of uniting the working class and resolving the deep social, economic and political inequalities and injustices inherent in this society, through collective action bridging the sectarian divide. Such an educational movement would act as a permanent beacon, a focus for social and political education in the Province and an inspiration to those in other western societies who are striving to create real alternatives in community education.

INDEX